Moab Classic Hikes
40 Hikes in the Moab Area

Written and photographed by Damian Fagan

Maps and illustrations by Lawrence Ormsby

CANYONLANDS
NATURAL HISTORY
ASSOCIATION

MOAB, UTAH

Table of Contents

Reprinted April, 2010

*To the memory of my father,
Lawrence J. Fagan, who helped
me follow my own path.*

Acknowledgments
Thanks to Andy Nettell of
Arches Book Company for
first suggesting this project,
and to Cindy Hardgrave of
the Canyonlands Natural
History Association for
bringing life to this guide. I
appreciate the proofreading
skills of Diane Allen, Katie
Stevens, Sam Wainer, and
Sena Hauer, as the text is
better for their review. I
would like to thank Sue
Bellagamba, Andrea Brand,
Jean McDowell, Murray
Shoemaker, Bill Stevens, and
the Moab Information
Center staff for their patience
and willingness to entertain
my barrage of questions. As
always, for my girls— Raven,
Luna and Jessie—for their
constant love and support.

Project coordinated by Cindy
Hardgrave, Executive
Director, CNHA

Design, maps and illustrations by Lawrence Ormsby
and Carole Thickstun,
www.ormsbythickstun.com

DEAD HORSE POINT
STATE PARK

Detail of Moab & Arches National Park Areas

COLORADO RIVER

PARK

128

16

15

Castle Valley Road

CASTLE VALLEY

SAND
FLATS
RECREATION
AREA

11

12 12

13

B

MANTI
LA SAL
NATIONAL
FOREST

7

Detail of Dead Horse Point State Park Area

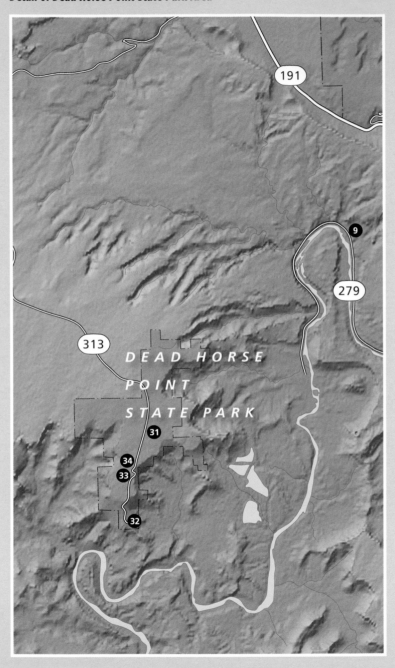

Detail of La Sal Mountains Area

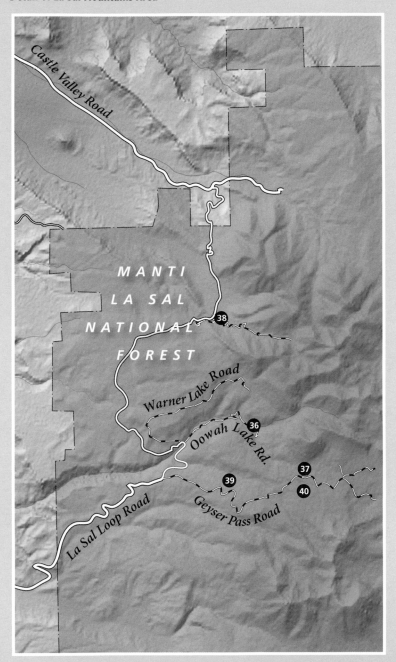

ALL ABOUT HIKING IN THE MOAB COUNTRY

In *The National Parks*, Freeman Tilden writes, "I would describe Canyonlands as the place where the adjective died from exhaustion." Spectacular, awesome, incredible, unbelievable—just a few of the common ones. Though he was referring to the park itself, the quote holds true for all of southern Utah. Dominated by high plateaus, sheer cliff walls, rock spires, and entrenched canyons, the area's cultural and natural history provides an intriguing foreground to the scenic background. This guide strives to present this blend of history and nature visible along the trail.

History lies fertile upon this land, from the immigration of Native Americans from the Great Plains or Canada, to the first European explorers. Following in their footsteps came the mountain men, outlaws, miners, and pioneers finding an untainted landscape. Settlements and towns blossomed like spring wildflowers, but have either faded into the dusty pages of history or fruited into the towns of today.

Covering forty trails within forty miles (as the raven flies) of Moab, Utah, *Moab Classic Hikes* introduces trails in Arches National Park, Dead Horse Point State Park, the La Sal Mountains, the City of Moab, and on lands managed by the U.S. Bureau of Land Management, including the Sand Flats Recreational Area. These are established, marked trails, not cross-country routes. Many of these trails are suitable for children to hike.

With Moab as the epicenter, the eleven area sections radiate outward like spokes on a wheel. Within the eleven sections are trail descriptions with cultural and natural history information pertinent to that hike, along with the particulars of access, mileage and difficulty. Much of the natural history information applies to the region, not just one particular trail. Remember that wildlife viewing is better morning and evening, and that wildflower displays vary each season depending upon winter and spring precipitation.

Land Administration

A majority of the trails in this book cross lands administered by the Moab Field Office of the Bureau of Land Management. The rest fall under jurisdiction of Arches National Park, Dead Horse Point State Park, The Nature Conservancy, U.S. Forest Service and the City of Moab. The diversity of the land managing agencies reflects different missions and regulations. This guide will provide you with some of those regulations, but you should be aware of the rules and regulations for each agency. This list does not include camping fees.

AGENCY	FEES	DOGS ON TRAIL	TRAIL USE[a]		
			Bicycles	Hikers	Jeeps/ATVs/ Motorcycles
Bureau of Land Management (BLM) and Manti La Sal National Forest (USFS)	No	Yes, under control and leashed in a campground	Yes	Yes	Yes
Arches National Park	Yes	No	No	Yes	No
BLM/Grand County Sand Flats Recreation Area	Yes	Yes, under control and leashed in a campground	Yes	Yes	Yes
City of Moab	No	Yes, leashed	Yes	Yes	No
Dead Horse Point State Park	Yes	Yes, leashed	No	Yes	No
The Nature Conservancy's Moab Rim Preserve	No	Yes, leashed	Yes	Yes	Yes
The Nature Conservancy's Scott Matheson Wetlands Preserve	No	No	No	Yes	No

[a] Check trail descriptions; some trails are posted hiking only. All bicycles, jeeps, motorcycles, and ATVs are restricted to designated routes.

For additional information about these agencies, see the Appendix section for contact numbers and websites.

Hiking with Children

Hiking is a great recreational past time. "The goal is the path" is my motto, not "The destination is the goal." That way I can smell the flowers along the trail, look for aquatic critters, bird watch, observe animal behavior, check on the clouds, and go "kid speed" if needed.

Hiking with children offers unique challenges and rewards. You know your child's abilities and needs better than anyone. Some kids sprint down the trail, then want to be carried back. Others go snail speed. Some like to check out everything, others want you to move faster.

A combination of snack stops, water breaks, nature investigations, and reasonable expectations will help you get down the trail. Treasure hunts, I-Spy, movement games (hopping, big steps, follow-the-leader), and hide-and-seek should be included in the adult version of the Ten Essentials. Make the hike fun, and you'll have a willing walking partner on your next outing.

Pre-Hike Planning

A little planning and preparation might represent the breaking point between a fun outing and a disaster. Don't just think of the current conditions—a pleasant July morning can turn blistering in the afternoon—and be aware of changing weather and attitudes. Be responsible for yourself and attuned to others. It is better to speak up and suggest a stop for water or another look at the map, than be spoken about at a later date.

Whether it is just grabbing a water bottle or filling a daypack, your destination will determine your pre-planning. Here are a few considerations before you head out.

✦ **Got H^{2}O.** Temperature, activity and fitness are three factors that contribute to heat-related problems. Drink sufficient quantities of water or liquids (not counting caffeine or sodas) to meet your physical needs. My rule of thumb is one quart per mile per person, more in warmer weather.

✦ **Good Shoes.** I've seen high heels click across slickrock, but I can't think of anything more painful. Select comfort and your feet will love you later.

✦ **Clothes.** A good layering system where you add or remove clothes to maintain a comfortable body temperature is key.

✦ **Pack a Pack.** A day pack or fanny pack is a good way to carry your stuff. Even when my daughter was very young, she wore a small fanny pack that could carry a doll, a snack and her water.

✦ **Food.** Provide trail snacks or picnics. Keep the kids and thus yourself happy—bring something to eat while on the trail. Another good idea is to leave a small cooler with iced drinks in the car—nothing better after a summer stroll.

✦ **Emergency Kit.** Trauma and disasters aside, I carry a small emergency kit with the following: bandages, antihistamine capsules, two bandanas, a pair of tweezers, a pocketknife, a flashlight, toilet paper, small ziplock bag, and waterproof matches. A small first-aid kit is handy, especially on longer hikes or if you tend to be accident-prone. There are great pre-made kits available.

✦ Sun Block/Lip Block. Protection from the sun can prevent painful sunburns. Reapply often.

✦ Hat that Cat. I might forget food, but never a hat. Winter warmth, summer shade. A good pair of polarizing sunglasses accompanies the hat.

✦ The Kitchen Sink. Maybe not, but certainly anything else you might need. My list might run: camera, film, small notebook, pencil, binoculars, map, dog leash, extra clothes, compass, GPS unit, map, field guides, etc. This list will vary per person and with the expected conditions. People who wear contacts or glasses might consider throwing in a spare pair— once I hiked a half-blind man out of a canyon in the dark because he lost a contact lens to a wayward branch.

✦ Insect Repellant. Gnats, mosquitoes and deer flies are the three main biting insects from which you might want protection. There are a number of repellants, both herbal and chemical, on the market. Long sleeves, pants or head nets may be necessary when conditions get fierce.

✦ Pets. Be responsible for your dog on the trail. Carry water for them, have a leash handy, check their feet often, and clean up their waste. Do not allow them to chase or harass wildlife or other hikers. Remember that dogs are not allowed on trails in the National Parks.

Trail Markers to Hazards: What to Watch For

Though this book covers established trails in the Moab area sometimes things happen. You never know when it might be your turn to ask for assistance. Even experienced hikers can turn an ankle or miss an over-hanging ledge. Pay attention to new surroundings or changing conditions. Here are a few reminders about trail markers and natural hazards.

✦ Cairns. These small piles of rock often mark the route. Sight the next one before proceeding. The Fins & Things trail has white dinosaurs painted on the slickrock to mark that trail. Canyon hikes such as Courthouse Wash or Hunter Canyon do not have trail markers but the canyon walls restricts these trails to the wash bottom.

✦ Slickrock. Appropriately named. When ice, snow, rain, or sand grains cover the surface, watch your footing. It may feel like you are walking on marbles.

✦ Ledges and Ledges. From small uneven ledges to thousand-foot cliffs, be aware of vertical drops or overhanging ledges.

✦ Plants and Animals. "If it doesn't sting, stick or stab you, watch out for its bite," so the saying goes. Scorpions and bee stings can trigger allergic reactions; imbedded cactus spines or yucca leaves really hurt; and cute chipmunks or buzzing rattlesnakes could result in a trip to the emergency room. Enjoy the flora and fauna but from a safe distance.

✦ Biological Soil Crust. Formerly known as cryptogamic crust or cryptobiotic soil, this living (hence the "biological" name) groundcover is the dark, lumpy soil crust found throughout the region; young crusts are nearly invisible. Composed of cyanobacteria, lichens, mosses, green algae, microfungi, and liverworts that live in the surface layer of desert soils, these organisms help "hold the place in place." This living crust stabilizes loose soils, stores water and nutrients, and changes atmospheric nitrogen into a form useful for plants. These crusts are easily destroyed by compaction; the impacted areas may take years to recover. Stay on trails or roads, or walk in washes or across the slickrock to minimize your impact on these important living communities.

✦ Changing Weather. Wind gusts, lightning, flash floods, oh my! Keep an eye on inclement weather and seek shelter when and where appropriate.

✦ Split Personalities. Drastic changes in a person's mood might not be due to multiple personalities; these can be the signs of physical discomfort or the need for medical care. Many of us don't express our discomfort until we are in bad shape—use your words to alert your hiking companions of any problems.

SCORPION ON BOOT

✦ Artifacts and Rock Art. Consider the prehistoric artifacts and rock art panels to be outdoor museum pieces: there for the admiring, but not for the touching. Federal law prohibits disturbance or removal of artifacts or rock art, so be considerate of future hikers and leave artifacts in place.

✦ Staying Lost/Getting Found. If you happen to lose the trail on your walk or become disoriented, the best things to do are STOP and RELAX. Do not panic, as fear is the mind-killer. Get your bearings by looking for familiar landmarks or features, listening for vehicles or other people, or checking your map. Think self-rescue, but don't try to scale sheer cliffs or take unnecessary risks to get back on the trail. If you are really lost, the saying "Staying Lost/Getting Found" means stay in one place, wait (pull out the cell phone or give an occasional shout), and you will be found.

Average Monthly Temperature and Rainfall Chart

In general, the climate in Moab tends towards cold winters and hot, dry summers. This chart reflects average Moab temperatures and precipitation throughout the year. Sometimes a single thunderstorm in July might equal the monthly average. Summer temperatures over 100° F are not uncommon. Don't ask, "When will the wind stop?" or "Is it always this hot here?" because you might not get a straightforward answer. Your pre-planning will help you deal with the weather.

Using This Guide

Designed for the casual hiker, this guide introduces forty hiking trails in and around the Moab area. All are well-marked trails, not cross-country routes. Included in each description are entries on general location, trail-head, mileage, and difficulty, as well as information about the natural and cultural wonders along that particular trail.

Organized by area, each section has an overview map that provides the location for each trail in that area. Included with each description is a trail map. These maps should be sufficient if you are hiking the marked trails. For additional information about roads and trails in the Moab area, the Moab West and Moab East waterproof maps produced by Latitude 40° Inc. are an excellent bargain. At a 1:75,000 scale, these two durable shaded relief maps should cover your adventure needs in the greater Moab area.

NOTE: *Some of the hikes in this book are on shared-use trails—note the bike or jeep icon indicating this use. That means that mountain bikes, motorcycles or four-wheel-drive vehicles may be encountered on these routes. During Jeep Safari Week, Spring Break, or Fat Tire Festival, these routes may be crowded with bikes or vehicles. If encountering vehicles on your hike does not appeal, select another trail and leave these for the off-season. Even though these are shared-use trails, they offer great walking opportunities.*

	Jan	Feb	Mar	Apr	May
Average High Temp °F	49	50	61	72	82
Average Low Temp °F	18	26	34	41	49
Average Precip. Inches	0.53"	0.62"	0.71"	0.88"	0.68"

The Rocks Speak

Sedimentary rock rules in Moab. Like a gigantic multi-tiered cake, each layer represents a slice of geologic history, and provides a glimpse into the long-distant past. These pages of time, recorded within the chapters of each geologic formation, tell an amazing story. Recorded in these formations are Sahara-like sand dunes, shallow seas filled with marine organisms, and temperate forests braided with slow-moving streams. Bones and tracks of dinosaurs, fossilized plants, coastal coral, and even the teeth of ocean-dwelling sharks exist within these layers.

Each layer is named for a location where the layer's unique characteristic is best expressed, and after the formation's composition. Hence, the Wingate Sandstone is named for Fort Wingate, New Mexico. Its composition is sandstone. Alternately, the multi-hued Morrison Formation bears the identity of Morrison, Colorado, while the word formation signifies the presence of several different rock types, in this case shales and sandstones.

The stratigraphic illustration reflects the arrangement and general topography of these formations. Erosion of these layers tends to result in characteristic features: sheer Wingate cliffs, arches and fins of the Entrada Formation, rounded hills of Mancos Shale. Included in the different trail descriptions is information about geologic formations pertinent to each hike.

Jun	Jul	Aug	Sep	Oct	Nov	Dec
93	99	96	87	74	57	45
57	63	62	52	40	28	21
0.45"	0.69"	0.88"	0.75"	1.08"	0.71"	0.65"

A Brief Glimpse of Moab History

Prehistoric Times

During the twilight years of the Pleistocene (roughly 1.8 million to ·10,000 years ago and generally referred to as the Ice Age) the climate on the Colorado Plateau was wetter and cooler than it is today. Mountain dwelling trees like limber pine and Douglas fir grew at lower elevations than they do today. Glaciers clung to the high slopes of the La Sals, and megafauna like the Columbia mammoth, American mastodon, giant sloth, American bison, Harrington's mountain goat, and Yesterday's camel roamed the lush valleys below. Fossil remains of these Ice Age fauna have been excavated from packrat middens within protected alcoves or dry caves. True to their names, pack rats haul bits of bone and plant material into the deeper recess of their caves, often embedding this material within thick layers of their feces and urine. Modern-day paleontologists tease apart these layers to uncover the evidence—horns, bones, teeth, tusks, antlers, pollen grains, seeds, pine needles, or intact dung balls, called boluses, to recreate a snapshot of the past.

About 11,000-12,000 years ago, coinciding with the extinction of many of these large megafauna, Ice Age hunters or Paleo-Indian were present on the Colorado Plateau. Little evidence remains of these nomadic big-game hunters. As the climate became warmer and drier, it is thought that the Paleo-Indians migrated out of the Colorado Plateau following the bison herds onto the Great Plains.

Early Inhabitants—Archaic and Ancestral Puebloans

Around 8,000-10,000 years ago, another hunter/gatherer culture named the Archaic moved into the region. Without the Pleistocene megafauna to hunt, these early inhabitants relied upon plants and smaller game— bighorn, deer, elk, and rabbits—than their Ice Age predecessors. Their tools included small projectile points, nets and snares made from braided yucca fibers and the atlatl—a throwing stick used to launch a spear. Stylized rock art, found throughout the area, is attributed to this culture.

With an increasing reliance upon agriculture, these Archaic nomads turned to a more sedentary life style between 2000 B.C. and A.D. 500. Corn, and later beans and squash, provided them with staple crops to supplement their diets of wild game and plants. Along with this cultural change came modifications in social structure, tools and utensils, storage shelters, and dwellings. Archaeologists trace the changes from and within basketry to pottery, atlatl to bow and arrow, pithouses to cliff dwellings, as well as changes in rock art styles.

The post Archaic culture, now called the Ancestral Puebloans (the older term "Anasazi" is a Navajo word roughly defined as "Ancient Ones" or "Enemy Elders"), stretched for about a thousand years here in southern

Utah. Though there aren't major cliff dwelling sites like Chaco Canyon or Mesa Verde here in Moab, evidence of these people exists through rock art sites, artifacts, and unearthed structures.

One of the great mysteries of the Colorado Plateau is why these people left their homelands, leaving behind tools, pottery and ancestors. A prolonged drought in the late 13th century is often cited as the reason that these people moved farther south into the Rio Grande Valley, joining other groups to form the modern-day Pueblo tribes.

As a perspective, here is another version from the April 7, 1905 *Grand Valley Times*. An exploration party was sent out by the Salt Lake Commercial Club to ascertain and explore the region of southeastern Utah between the Abajo Mountains and the San Juan River. The article "The Exploring Party Pass Through Moab," describes the area and the people as "....a region that was in prehistoric times the home of many thousands of the cliff dweller race....These people are evidently co-temporaneus with the ancient Egyptians and were possibly a branch of that race cut off from communications with them when the lost continent Atlantis went down." Oh, really!

Precisely when the ancestors of the modern-day tribes—Ute, Paiute, and Navajo arrived in the Moab area is speculative. There are references to the "Yutas" in Spanish historical records dating to the 1600s. In 1765 the Spanish expedition led by Juan María Antonio de Rivera documented the historical encounter of Spaniards and Utes in the Moab area. The crossing for the Colorado River was, back then, known as the Ute Crossing.

Old Spanish Trail

In the 1700s, Spain claimed the southwestern region of the current United States. To connect Spanish settlements in California with missions in New Mexico, and to gain better control of the region, Spanish expeditions explored trails west from New Mexico and east from California. From New Mexico, the Rivera expedition in 1765, and in 1776 the Fray Francisco Atanasio Dominguez and Fray Silvestre Velez de Escalante's expedition entered southern Utah and southwestern Colorado, but never found a route to California.

In 1826, mountain man Jedediah Smith pioneered a route from the Great Salt Lake to southern California, using some of the earlier Spanish explorers' trails. A Mexican trader, Antonio Armijo, in 1829, led the first pack trip across this 1,100-mile trail from New Mexico to California. One of the darker chapters of the trail's history involved the trading or selling of Indian slaves to the Spanish traders.

Leaving New Mexico in the fall, traders would pack woolen blankets, rugs, and cloth to exchange for mules, horses, and goods from California.

The two-month return journey began in early spring before snowmelt made the rivers too deep to cross. Along either trip, Paiute or Ute Indians traded captives for horses, and these slaves might end up in California, New Mexico or Mexico. Trail use was highest from 1829 to 1848; the United States obtained lands under Mexican claim after the Mexican-American War. The trail saw little use after 1848, since it was no longer the main route to California. Today, this route is a National Historic Trail.

Elk Mountain Mission and Early Settlement

Mountain men and fur trappers passed through Spanish Valley prior to the settlers. One of these trappers, Denis Julien, left inscriptions in Arches National Park and at several spots along the Green River. On May 7, 1855, a group of 41 Mormon men left Salt Lake City to establish a mission in the upper portion of the valley. Led by Alfred W. Billings, this mission is known as the Billings Party or Elk Mountain Mission, for at that time, the La Sals were known as the Elk Mountains. The party followed portions of the Spanish Trail to Moab. The group planted gardens and built a rock fort, but troubles between the Mormons and the local Utes resulted in the Mormons retreating back to Salt Lake City after a stay of several months.

After the United States negotiated a treaty with the Utes in 1872, hostilities between the Native Americans and the settlers lessened, although conflicts still arose such as the Pinhook Battle of 1881. This treaty provided an opening for settlers who came to the valley in search of good grazing and farming land, while prospectors searched for silver or gold. Numerous canyons or features bear the names of these early settlers.

With increased settlement came improvements in transportation and infrastructure. In 1880, settlers wanted a Post Office established in the valley. The name Moab, meaning "the far country," was selected for the town, and a petition to change the name to "Vina" a decade later, failed. Grand County, formed in 1890, was named after the Grand River (later changed to the Colorado River) that cut across the north end of Little Grand Valley. You will hear the names Moab Valley and Spanish Valley used interchangeably. But on topographical maps Moab Valley covers most of the northern portion including Old Town (the downtown area), while Spanish Valley represents the southern half of the valley. Though Moab was platted in 1884, it did not incorporate until 1902.

The newspaper *Grand Valley Times* rolled off the presses starting in 1896. In the editor's "Salutations" column, he writes, "In making an appearance to the people of southeastern Utah we have no apology to offer. The newspaper has become a necessary factor in the age of civilization." Now the local gatherings had printed material to gossip about.

A narrow gauge rail line of the Denver and Rio Grande Western Railroad provided better access to cattle markets for the area ranchers. The thirty-five mile wagon trip from Moab to the rail stop at Thompson Springs took over eight hours to complete. A halfway stage station, operated near Courthouse Rock, allowed travelers a respite during their journey.

As mineral exploration increased, mining towns sprouted like mushrooms after a rain in the La Sals. Speculators called it a "bonanza," as they tried to lure gold rush seekers to Utah. Oil and gas exploration resulted in gushers and dry holes. Uranium, mined as early as 1871 for ceramic glazing, ink dyes and the manufacturing of steel plate, had periodic episodes of profitability, but nothing compared to the post-World War II boom.

Dawn of the 20th century unveiled a developing frontier town, with an agricultural identity. The publisher of the *Grand Valley Times*, Justin Corbin, wrote, "…bicycles are becoming common on Moab streets…" in his June 21, 1901 edition. How little did he suspect.

Starting in the early 1900s, tourism was a minor industry that hovered around the economic edges of Moab. Though the designation of Arches National Monument in 1929 gave the area a small boost, tourism would not catch on until after World War II.

In the early 1900s, farms and small ranches dotted the valley, but fruit production ruled the day. Prize-winning apples, peaches, grapes, and pears were harvested and hauled to the railroad depot at Thompson for distribution to California and elsewhere. A fruit growers association formed in 1906, and a canning factory was built in 1911. At peak production the plant employed twenty people; many current-day neighborhoods have remnant fruit trees from this era.

MOAB COOPERATIVE CO., 1919

Transportation was always an issue. In 1902, the steamboat *Undine* traveled from Green River to Moab and back over a ten-day period. Unfortunately, the steamboat overturned. A road was constructed along the Colorado River upstream towards Dewey. Opened in 1902, the road suffered from high water flooding. A boulder along Highway 128, upstream of Hittle Bottom, announces this stretch as the Kings Toll Road, after its creator Samuel King. The sentiment of the day was summed up in a letter to the *Grand Valley Times* editor in 1896 by Sylvester Richardson: "Moab should extend roads, and good ones in every direction if she wishes to prosper beyond a certain limit…"

In 1909, the first automobile entered into the Moab Valley, driven by tourists W.E. Cameron and his son. Driving from the train station at Thompson Springs along the wagon road to the Colorado River north of town took a reported three and one-half hours. After being ferried across the river, the visitors provided rides to the locals.

The 1920s saw a shift from agriculture towards mineral exploration. Coal mining and oil drilling had occurred sporadically for the past twenty years, but the *Times-Independent* proclaimed in the January 22, 1920 issue, that due to the current drilling activity "Oil is King in Moab Valley." In 1925 the Frank Shafer (for whom the Shafer Trail in Canyonlands National Park is named) No. 1 well became the county's first gusher. Again, the cycle of boom and bust followed, and by the close of the 1920s, the oil industry had slowed down.

Arches National Monument, dedicated in 1929, covered 4,520 acres. Driving the rough Willow Springs entrance road was half the excitement of getting "to the Arches." Alex Ringhoffer, "Doc" Williams, Loren "Bish" Taylor, and other locals were instrumental in the establishment of the monument.

In the 1930s, Senator Frank Moss proposed a huge 4.5-million-acre national monument—the Escalante National Monument—that would encompass most of southern Utah. Backed by Secretary of the Interior Harold Ickes, the plan ran into major opposition. Conservative factions did not support the idea of locking up potential developable lands, and with leeriness towards the federal government, the plan was shelved in 1938.

In the late 1940s, the powerful Atomic Energy Commission sparked an explosion of exploration in southern Utah. With a guaranteed base price for uranium in 1950, Moab evolved from an agricultural-based fruit and ranching community into a prospector's town. Charlie Steen, a geologist and prospector, struck pay dirt with the Mi Vida claim, south of La Sal in July 1952. A year later, the town's population started to climb; within three years the population would quadruple. Those were wild days with prospectors and investors fueling the uranium frenzy. Roads were bulldozed to provide access to developing claims; many of these roads would form the foundation for mountain biking trails starting in the mid 1980s.

Steen and other investors built a uranium processing mill on the north bank of the Colorado River that would process the uranium ore. Business was good and Moab boasted of being the "Uranium Capital of the World." Tent villages sprouted like weeds, and many of the orchards that once supported the agricultural industry became housing developments. Oil and natural gas exploration, service-related businesses and the fledgling tourist industry were also growing during this period. Utilizing military surplus rafts, river runners rowed tourists down the rapids of the Green and Colorado rivers.

The 1960s and 1970s saw growth and decline in the mineral and oil and gas industry. The Texas Gulf Sulphur Company switched from conventional mining to solution mining at its Potash Plant. Solution mining involved pumping underground briny solution into evaporation ponds on the surface. Potash and salt (sodium chloride) were transported from the plant, via the railroad spur, to national and international markets. Meanwhile, tourism was knocking on the door as the next growing economic sector, taking over the reins from the slumping mining industry. With the dedication of Canyonlands National Park in 1964, and Arches transformed from a national monument into a national park on November 16, 1971, recreational interest in the area began to grow.

Sometime in the late 1970s, a bicycle with fat tires rolled into Moab. What a great idea, people thought—now we don't have to ride our road bikes on the dirt roads. The mountain biking boom was about to explode.

As the glow of atomic energy faded, the mines and mills started closing. By the mid 1980s, the uranium frenzy was just about over. Conflicts between federal land management agencies and local political forces arose, as the economic mainstays of mining and ranching began to decline. Though just a rural town in southern Utah, Moab felt the economic impacts of global industrial markets, as well as the increased scrutiny of urban and international recreationalists. As the mining boom faded, tourism and the associated service industries carried Moab from the depths of economic despair to the universal popularity of today. With an advertising ploy to boost the economy and gain national attention, Moab hosted the "World's Most Scenic Dump" contest.

Moab's past has been a roller coaster ride of boom and bust cycles. Today, Moab's economy is a mixture of tourism, services, ranching, oil and gas, commercial filming, telecommuters, and government. What legacies will the history books record about this town in the future is a question that bears discussion. Meanwhile, the sandstone cliffs bear silent witness to the ever-changing saga in the Moab Valley.

Kane Creek Boulevard intersects with U.S. Highway 191 just south of the Moab Information Center. This road follows the Colorado River from the Portal, where the river enters a steep-walled canyon, and flows downstream towards Kane Creek Canyon. The pavement ends at Pritchett Canyon, but the maintained dirt road into Kane Creek Canyon to the Hunter Canyon trailhead is passable to a two-wheel-drive vehicle (under normal conditions). Beyond Hunter Canyon, clearance and four-wheel-drive are recommended.

SIDE-BLOTCHED LIZARD

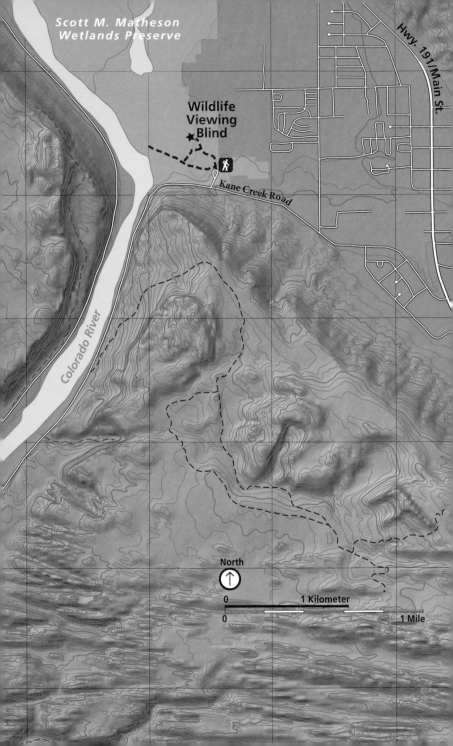

I Scott M. Matheson Wetlands Preserve

Trailhead: Located at 934 Kane Creek Boulevard. From U.S. 191, turn west onto Kane Creek Boulevard and continue 0.9 mile to the parking area.

Mileage: 1.0-mile round-trip, wheelchair accessible.

Difficulty: Easy.

The Scott M. Matheson Wetlands Preserve, co-owned by The Nature Conservancy and the Utah Division of Wildlife Resources, is a lush, flooded bottomland along the Colorado River. Locally known as "The Sloughs," the preserve is a green oasis in a land of redrock.

Groundwater and irrigation returns feed the 890-acre wetland, as does the Colorado River during spring runoff when the river exceeds 40,000 cubic feet per second (cfs) and overbank flooding occurs.

The riparian and wetland habitats here offer outstanding opportunities for wildlife watching. More than 225 species of birds have been observed in the preserve; mid-April to late May is the best bird watching season. Other species of wildlife that roam the preserve are mule deer, striped skunk, beaver, gray fox, muskrat, raccoon, northern leopard frog, bullfrog, and western garter snake.

The one-mile trail forms a loop through the southern portion of the preserve. A compacted soil trail connects with the boardwalk constructed of recycled redwood from an old railroad trestle that once spanned the Great Salt Lake. There are benches and a viewing blind that invite visitors to stop and observe activity in the wetlands.

Members of the early Elk Mountain Mission built their fort near the wetlands on the east side of Moab. Subsequent owners used the sloughs to graze livestock or harvest cottonwoods for fence posts and firewood. Back in the early 1900s if you wanted ice delivered to your home, you had to specify either "Goose Island" or "Swamp" ice from the sloughs.

Notes: Although there is an active mosquito abatement program in the preserve, expect and be prepared for mosquitoes from April through September.

Ditches and dikes were built to drain the wetlands and prevent flooding from the Colorado River during spring runoff. The river would divert these changes during years of overbank flooding. Seasonal and annual changes make this a dynamic area; some years the ponds dry up, other years the boardwalk trail is under flood waters from the Colorado River.

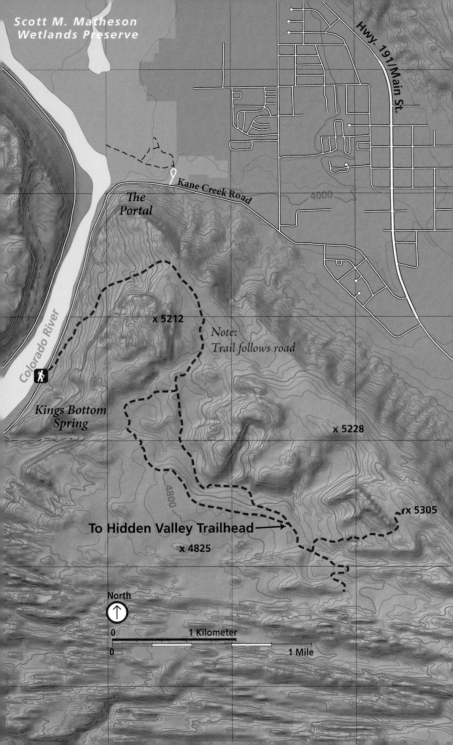

2 Moab Rim Trail

Trailhead: 2.6 miles from U.S. 191 along Kane Creek Boulevard.

Mileage: 1.4 miles one-way to overlook; 3.0 miles one-way to Hidden Valley Trail connection. There are painted white stripes on the rocks that mark the trail.

Difficulty: Steep trail; moderate to difficult.

Locally known as the "Moab Stairmaster," this hike follows a rough four-wheel-drive road up the slickrock to several points of interest. Used mostly by four-wheel-drive vehicles and hikers, you may encounter heavy traffic on this shared-use trail, especially during Jeep Safari Week.

Sheer cliffs of Navajo Sandstone tower above the trail. Hikers follow the blackened trail of tire marks up the slickrock ramps and across the stone ledges to the overlook. The trail winds across private property to incredible vantage points of the Moab/Spanish Valley, Matheson Preserve, and La Sal Mountains. Past the private section, the trail continues to other overlooks and accesses the BLM-managed Behind-the-Rocks Wilderness Study Area. One spur continues to the south to a pass where the Moab Rim Trail connects with the Hidden Valley Trail. At the pass, there are numerous rock art images pecked into the sandstone wall. Hikers and mountain bikers may proceed from this pass south to Hidden Valley; motorcycles, ATVs, and vehicles are not permitted past this point.

Some hikers may wish to shuttle a vehicle to either the Hidden Valley Trailhead or the Moab Rim Trailhead, in order to hike this trail one-way. On certain weekends in spring and fall, this trail can be very crowded with four-wheel-drive enthusiasts. The Nature Conservancy purchased the private land section that includes the overlook. They removed the passenger tram operation, as well as closed the off-road side trails and the rock crawler trail to motorized vehicles. This area is now known as the Moab Rim Preserve, and is managed in cooperation with the BLM.

DWARF EVENING PRIMROSE
Oenothera caespitosa

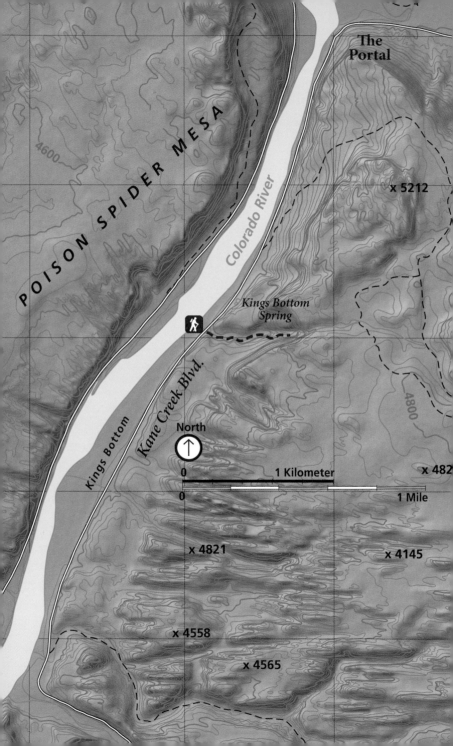

The Portal

x 5212

POISON SPIDER MESA

4600

Colorado River

Kings Bottom Spring

Kings Bottom

Kane Creek Blvd.

4800

North

0   1 Kilometer

0   1 Mile

x 482

x 4821

x 4145

x 4558

x 4565

3 Moonflower Canyon

Trailhead: 3.0 miles from the intersection of U.S. 191 along Kane Creek Boulevard.
Mileage: 1.0 mile round-trip.
Difficulty: Easy.

This is a short box canyon that ends at a vertical pour off 0.5 mile from the parking area. The trail passes eight campsites located in the mouth of the canyon.

Named for the sacred daturas or moonflowers (*Datura wrightii*) that grow here, these relatives of tobacco have large trumpet-shaped white flowers that bloom from evening to morning. Sphinx moths, which may be mistaken for small hummingbirds, are nocturnal pollinators attracted to the nectar produced by the flowers. The flowers curl up in the day, resembling hand-rolled cigars. The plant produces toxic alkaloids (atropine, scopolamine, and hyoscyamine) as protection against herbivores. Native Americans, for ceremonial purposes, harvested the leaves and seeds for their narcotic properties; modern day misuse has led to injury and death associated with the plant's hallucinogenic properties.

CAVE PRIMROSE
Primula specuicola

The primitive trail follows the canyon bottom, past large cottonwood trees and groves of gnarled Gambel's oak. Several different wildflowers grow along the wash, notably the red-flowered Indian paintbrush and scarlet gilia. The small alcove by campsite six contains a hanging garden—literally where plants cling to the cliff wall, their roots finding footholds beneath flakes of sandstone. Cave Primrose, also know as the Easter flower (*Primula specuicola*) has a small pinkish-purple flower with a yellow center, and is named after its seasonal flowering period. Later on in the season, troops of scarlet Eastwood's monkey-flowers (*Mimulus eastwoodiae*) color this alcove. Beware of the poison ivy (*Toxicodendron rydbergii*) with the shiny green leaves in clusters of three. The large glossy leaves and stems contain urshinol oil that may cause skin irritations or rashes. Avoid contact with the plant and don't let your dog run through the poison ivy. Oils adhere to their fur, which may then transfer to your hand upon petting or handling your dog.

A small spring-fed pond exists at the end of the trail and is a cool respite from summer's heat. During rainstorms, runoff from the Behind-the-Rocks area, above and to the south of the pour-off, creates spectacular waterfalls and potential flash floods into the canyon.

4 Pritchett Canyon

Trailhead: Located 4.8 miles from the intersection of U.S. 191 and Kane Creek Boulevard. The canyon entrance is on private property; the landowner charges a small fee for access.

Mileage: 9.0 miles round-trip.

Difficulty: Moderate to Difficult

The trailhead is on private property and there is a small entrance fee to enter the canyon. You can deposit your fee in the self-register box. Though there is a rough four-wheel-drive road in the canyon bottom, this can be a great hiking trail when there is little traffic on the road. Mountain bikers ride this trail and ascend out of the canyon at Yellow Hill, enroute to connecting with other trails.

Pritchett Canyon forms the west flank of the Behind-the-Rocks Wilderness Study Area. This is an area of incised canyons, sandstone fins, and high cliffs. Some of the side canyons offer explorations into this wilderness area; others end at inaccessible pour-offs.

Pritchett Canyon is named after Thomas Pritchett, an early settler in Moab. He lived in a fort in this canyon during the winter of 1880-1881. Pritchett was also the first Justice of the Peace in the valley, and he performed the first marriage ceremony in Moab back in 1881, but there isn't much recorded history about him.

Pritchett Canyon lacks a perennial water flow, but there may be pools of water in the canyon bottom. Lizards, desert cottontails, coyotes, and mule deer are just some of the wildlife species hikers may encounter in the canyon. Canyon and rock wrens also occur in the canyon. The song of the canyon wren is a descending whistle, while the rock wren's song is a short, buzzy trill. Rock wrens build a nest within a narrow rocky confine and pave the entrance way to the nest with small stones. Canyon wrens also nest in rocky areas, often selecting a nest site behind a protective slab of rock.

Prickly pear cacti (*Opuntia* sp.), with their rounded pads, grow on sandy slopes in the canyon. The colorful flowers and nectar attract a host of insect pollinators. Check out a flower to observe beetles or bees plowing through the numerous stamens inside the flower. The sweet, seedy fruits of the cactus have very fine spines to protect them, while the pads have larger spines to deter herbivores.

A scale insect called the cochineal bug lives on the pads beneath a downy shell that resembles a small white cotton ball. These insects were, and still are today, harvested and crushed to form a red dye.

POISON SPIDER MESA

AMASA BACK

North

0   1 Kilometer

0   1 Mile

Colorado River

Kings Bottom

Kane Creek Blvd.

Williams Bottom

Note:
Trail follows road

X 4660

X 4802

4785 X   X 4790

JACKSON HOLE

Jackson Bottom

KANE SPRINGS CANYON

5 Amasa Back

Trailhead: Located 6.0 miles from the intersection of U.S. 191 and Kane Creek Boulevard. A graded dirt parking lot, about ½ mile before the trailhead turnoff, provides better parking than the small pullouts near the trailhead.

Mileage: 9.0 miles round-trip.

Difficulty: Moderate to Difficult, elevation gain is over 1,000 feet.

The trail follows an old uranium exploration road to some spectacular views of the La Sal Mountains, Colorado River and Jackson's Hole (the abandoned river meander below where John Jackson grazed cattle and horses).

From the Kane Creek Boulevard, the trail/road descends to the creek. This is a rough four-wheel-drive road and air-catching mountain bike ride. Where the road crosses the creek at the bottom of the hill, you might have to wade the short distance to the opposite bank.

Mountain bikers attempting to cross Kane Creek sometimes provide entertainment as they misjudge the depth of the crossing and create spectacular crashes into the creek! At certain water flows you'll need to wade the creek. If you walk the creek barefooted, beware of loose or sharp rocks.

ROCK ART RESEMBLING AN OWL

Once on the other bank, look to the large arch-in-the-making alcove located at the base of the Navajo Sandstone wall to the north. Along the base of this wall are some interesting petroglyphs that resemble bighorn sheep, owls, and bird-like figures.

After the creek crossing, the road ascends the slope via a winding route until it reaches the high ridge. The route to the Colorado River overlook may seem a bit confusing, since there are several spur trails and roads leading from the main trail. The main trail to the overlook forks to the north and follows the spine of Amasa Back.

Amasa Back is named for George Amasa Larsen (1866-1947), a cattleman who arrived in Spanish Valley in 1880. Though Larsen could not read, he was regarded as a smart man. In the book *Grand Memories*, Larsen was remembered being able to "figure it faster in his head than anyone could with a paper and pencil." Amasa Back is a three-mile-long ridge, called a hogback, which extends above a bend of the Colorado River. At the overlook there are great bird's-eye-views of the Potash Plant, Colorado River and the Jackson Hole rincon.

x 4448

x 4845

HUNTER

x 4542

Kane Creek Road

x 5030

x 4588

CANYON

x 5041

x 5290

Kane Springs Creek

North

1 Kilometer

1 Mile

6 Hunter Canyon

Trailhead: 7.8 miles from the intersection of Kane Creek Boulevard and U.S. 191.
Mileage: 6.0 miles round-trip.
Difficulty: Moderate, brushy in sections.

The Hunter Canyon trail follows the canyon bottom, with frequent crossings of the intermittent spring-fed creek. Numerous aquatic insects, such as caddis flies, dragonfly and damselfly nymphs, water boatmen, mosquito larvae, and water striders can be observed in the pools. Red-spotted and Woodhouse's toads also breed in this canyon. The nighttime call of the red-spotted toad sounds like a high trill, while the male Woodhouse's call is a guttural *waaaaaa*, somewhat resembling a bleating sheep.

Young red-spotted toads are tiny ¹⁄₂ inch long and grayish in color with red spots. Adult toads average 1¹⁄₂-3 inches long (SVN—snout to vent), while the Woodhouse's toads are much larger at about four inches long (SVN). The toad's name honors Samuel Woodhouse, a U.S. Army Civil War surgeon and naturalist.

The streamside or riparian vegetation consists of tall Fremont cottonwoods, coyote willow, and tamarisk. Up on the drier banks are big sagebrush, Mormon tea and the white-flowered fendlerbush. The dense riparian habitat makes this another good bird watching site during spring and summer.

WOODHOUSE'S TOAD
Bufo woodhousei

One-half mile up the canyon from the trailhead, Hunter's Arch perches on the east canyon wall. White-throated swifts and violet-green swallows may be observed hawking insects in flight near this arch. The swifts have narrow pointed wings, and their white and black plumage makes them appear dressed in tuxedos. The swallows have more rounded wings and are white below. Both species build their nests beneath protective rock slabs high on canyon walls.

The narrow trail ends at a pour-off, although many hikers turn back before this point because of the dense vegetation in the canyon bottom.

COLLARED LIZARD

Locally known as "the Potash Road," Utah 279 follows the Colorado River downstream from Moab to the Potash Plant. Designated a Scenic Byway, even the drive alone is worth the effort. There are pullouts for viewing petroglyphs, dinosaur tracks and canyon scenery.

Potash deposits occur in the vast Paradox Formation that underlies the Four Corners region. The deposits are the remnants of ancient seas that once covered the area. As a major source of potassium, potash was first mined for its value as fertilizer. Started in 1964 as a traditional underground mining operation, the plant was modified in 1970, after an underground mining disaster, to a combination solution mining and solar evaporation system. Water pumped into the underground mine dissolves the potash salts, which are then piped to vinyl-lined shallow ponds on the surface. Here solar radiation evaporates the water, leaving behind the crystallized salts. The harvested salts are then transported to the plant for processing.

Between the Jaycee Park Recreation Site and the Poison Spider Trailhead, the road parallels high Wingate Sandstone cliffs. Several pullouts along this road provide parking from which to view the numerous rock art images on the cliffs or to watch the rock climbers ascend the corporate routes of "Wall Street." Be aware of the semi-truck traffic in this area, as there are only narrow shoulders between the road and the river.

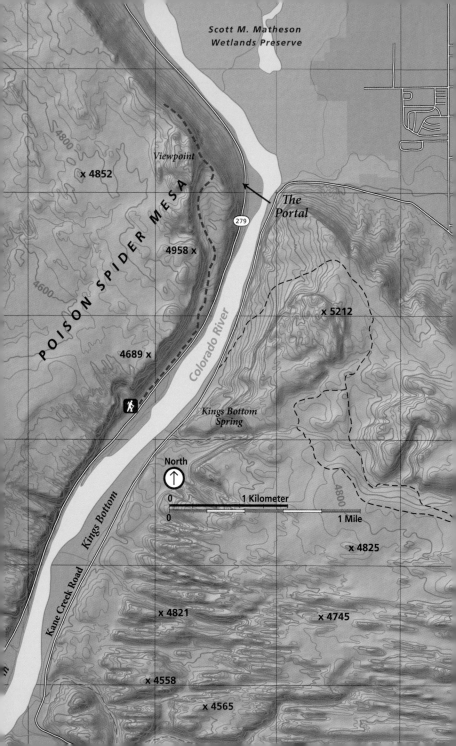

Scott M. Matheson
Wetlands Preserve

Viewpoint

x 4852

P O I S O N   S P I D E R   M E S A

4958 x

The
Portal

279

Colorado River

4689 x

x 5212

Kings Bottom
Spring

North

↑

0
1 Kilometer

0
1 Mile

x 4825

Kings Bottom

Kane Creek Road

x 4821

x 4745

x 4558

x 4565

7

Portal Overlook Trail

Trailhead: The Jaycee Park Recreation Site is 4.0 miles downstream on Utah 279 from its intersection with U.S. 191.

Mileage: 4.0 miles round-trip to Portal Overlook.

Difficulty: Moderate to difficult on this steep, rocky trail.

The hike to the Portal Overlook starts at the Jaycee Park, traverses along the base of the Wingate cliff, then follows a steep incline along a bedding plane of the Kayenta Formation to a spectacular, unfenced viewpoint. The overlook offers stunning views of the Moab/Spanish Valley, La Sal Mountains, Colorado River, and Scott M. Matheson Wetlands Preserve.

The massive buttresses of Poison Spider Mesa and the Moab Rim constrict the river's exit from the Moab Valley. This point is the Portal.

At several locations along the lower portion of the trail are large river cobbles that mark the ancestral channel deposits of the Colorado River—a stark contrast to the river's current location. These channel deposits include cobbles washed down from the nearby mountains, as well as material from Westwater Canyon, Glenwood Springs Canyon, and the Uncompahgre Highlands farther upstream in Colorado.

Along this trail you might encounter several different species of lizards that are common throughout Canyon Country. Side-blotched lizards, named for the dark spots behind their forelegs, are small sandstone-colored lizards with tiny white dorsal spots. Due to their small size they are able to thermoregulate faster; hence, these lizards are the first to emerge in spring and the last to enter into hibernation in winter. Western fence lizards or blue bellies also occur along this trail. Their dark metallic blue undersides help to identify these lizards. Both the side-blotched and fence lizards may fall prey to the larger long-nosed leopard lizard, a "leopard-spotted" lizard.

Note: Give way to mountain bikers descending this rough and rocky trail. The unmaintained trail continues past the overlook, below the sheer cliffs to the trail/road that connects to the Poison Spider Mesa trailhead. This trail is extremely precipitous and dangerous.

Other reptiles that may be encountered along the trail are western whiptail lizards or midget faded rattlesnakes. Whiptails eat ants and other insects; the rattlesnakes prefer small rodents. The warning system of the rattlesnake is a dry buzz, meant as a warning and to indicate their presence; these reclusive snakes may not rattle until you are in mid-stride above them. Their venom can be fatal, but the local hospital rarely treats a person for snakebite. Local veterinarians, however, do treat an occasional dog that has been bitten on the nose.

Decades ago, William Hinton rode his horses up this trail to access his cattle allotments atop Poison Spider Mesa, although some older maps label this area "Sand Flats." Some call this the "Hinton Trail." In the Personal Histories section of the *Daughters of Utah Pioneers' Grand Memories*, Hinton, at one time a deputy sheriff, is said to have been acquainted with outlaws Butch Cassidy, Matt Warner, Zak Light and others, as well as the famous sheriff Pat Garrett.

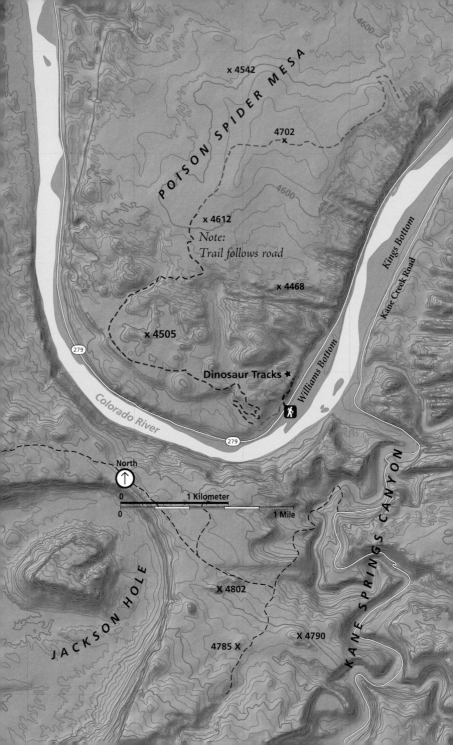

POISON SPIDER MESA

x 4542

4702
x

x 4612

Note:
Trail follows road

x 4468

x 4505

Dinosaur Tracks ★

Williams Bottom

Kings Bottom

Kane Creek Road

279

Colorado River

279

North
↑

0
0

1 Kilometer

1 Mile

KANE SPRINGS CANYON

JACKSON HOLE

X 4802

4785 X

X 4790

8 Poison Spider Mesa—Dinosaur Tracks

Trailhead: 5.9 miles downstream on Utah 279 from the junction with U.S. 191.
Mileage: 300 yards round-trip to dinosaur tracks, 8.2 miles one-way to Portal Rim.
Difficulty: Easy to Difficult.

The short unmaintained trail to the dinosaur tracks starts at the trailhead parking area and traverses across and up a series of rock ledges to a set of dinosaur tracks frozen in time. The three-toed tracks belong to an Allosaurus, a Jurassic period predator. The tracks were made in soft mud, and then covered over by other sediments. Compressed and cemented into rock, eventual erosion exposed these tracks to reveal evidence that these prehistoric creatures once roamed southern Utah.

The Poison Spider Mesa trail is a shared-use trail. Mountain bike, ATV, jeep, and motorcycle use is high on this route. You may prefer walking this road in the off-season when traffic is light or non-existent.

There are numerous forks and illegal off-road tracks in this area. Keep to the main road and follow the little jeep icons, not the spike icons (the spikes are for the Golden Spike Trail). The road crosses over numerous humps of Navajo Sandstone as it ascends towards the rim.

The Navajo Sandstone, like the Wingate, was a vast inland sand dune complex. Ephemeral lakes or playas formed in these dunes, so you might find a small lens of limestone within the sandstone. Named

DINOSAUR TRACKS IN A
ROCK SLAB

after Navajo Mountain, the type locality of this sandstone, the Navajo tends to erode into rounded cliffs or mounds.

NAVAJO SANDSTONE

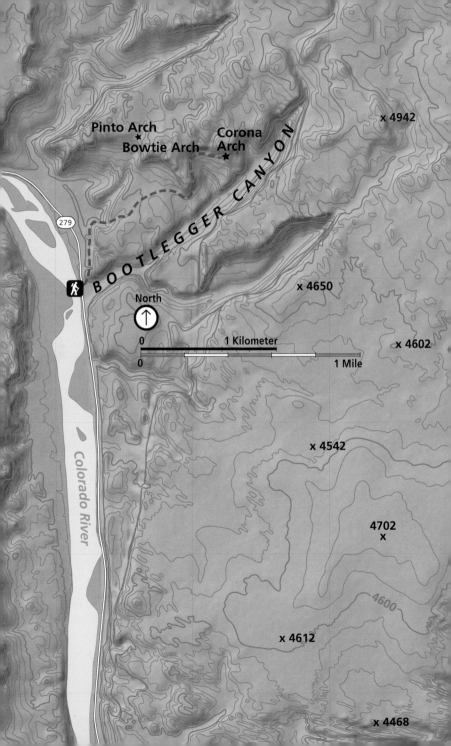

Pinto Arch
★
Bowtie Arch   Corona
★ Arch

BOOTLEGGER CANYON

279

x 4942

x 4650

North
↑

0
0

1 Kilometer

1 Mile

x 4602

x 4542

4702
x

4600

x 4612

Colorado River

x 4468

9 Corona Arch Trail

Trailhead: Across from the Gold Bar Campground, located 9.9 miles downstream on Utah 279 from the junction with U.S. 191.

Mileage: 3.0 miles round-trip.

Difficulty: Moderate.

Located at the end of a small canyon, Corona Arch resembles a sandstone halo. Eroded into a wall of Navajo Sandstone, Corona Arch was a staple on the nightly, local news. A short clip featured a small fixed-wing plane flying through the arch. Although the arch is bigger than it seems, this practice is no longer permitted.

From the parking lot, the trail ascends a short slope to the railroad tracks. You can see where the rocks were blasted for the tracks. The tracks pass through a mile-long tunnel in the cliff and continue northward by the Atlas Mill Site. Although train traffic is scarce, freight trains still use these tracks to haul potash from the plant to markets in California.

As you get closer to Corona Arch there are a couple of safety cables strung up along some exposed portions of the trail, as well as a series of steps cut into the slickrock and a short ladder to climb. Those with a fear of heights should stop just after the first cable section where there is a view of Corona and Bowtie arches.

High up in the Navajo Sandstone cliff, visible to the north of the main trail, is Bowtie Arch. Also known as Pinto Arch, this arch is a good example of a pothole arch, where water first eroded a large pothole or water tank atop the sandstone cliff. Additional chemical and mechanical erosion wore through the bottom of the pothole. The result is a hole in the bottom of the pothole. Subsequent erosion, sometimes due to rainstorm runoff, has enlarged this hole creating the arch you see today.

Past Bowtie Arch, the trail follows the slickrock slope to Corona Arch. The arch is sometimes referred to as Little Rainbow Bridge because of its resemblance to Rainbow Bridge on Lake Powell. From a distance the arch seems small, but the opening is 140 feet by 105 feet.

An abundance of wildflowers and flowering shrubs may color this trail. One species is the narrow-leaf yucca (*Yucca angustifolia*) with its tall wands of white flowers arising from a cluster of bayonet-like leaves. Native Americans harvested yucca leaves and made twine by twisting or plaiting together the strong fibers. This twine became sandals, snares, and rope, binding the people to this plant. Nocturnal moths called yucca moths pollinate the yuccas. In this symbiotic relationship, a female yucca moth collects pollen from one plant, which is rolled into a ball and transferred to a different yucca plant. There she inserts the pollen into the flower's stigma to pollinate the flower. The female also deposits her eggs in the base of the flower's ovary, where her larvae will feed upon some of the maturing seeds of the plant. Both plant and moth benefit from this relationship.

Home to the world-famous Slickrock Bike Trail, the Sand Flats Recreation Area stretches across a high plateau bordered by Negro Bill Canyon and Mill Creek. The Recreation Area encompasses 7,240 acres, and is managed through a unique partnership between BLM and Grand County. Access to the area is via the Sand Flats Road, which continues past the Recreation Area to the Porcupine Rim Trailhead, and eventually connects to the La Sal Mountain Loop Road.

Up until the early 1900s, when a road along the Colorado River was built, the main access to Castle Valley was via the Sand Flats Road and over Porcupine Rim to the valley. Back in 1890, John Martin (for which Mad Martin Point is named) and Herbert Day hauled a threshing machine from Moab to Castle Valley. Twelve horses pulled the rig up Sand Flats to Wilson Mesa, through Burkholder and Pinhook

Draw, and down to their ranch in Castle Valley. The adventure took them twenty days since they had to build portions of the road along the way.

The Sand Flats shared-use trails are open to bikes, four-wheel drives, and motorcycles, but hikers may also take advantage of these trails. There are spur roads along most routes, so be aware of your location. Vehicular trail use varies by season and time of day, so check with the Sand Flats staff for hiking suggestions. Spring, fall, and off-season holidays are the busiest times on the trails. Many locals hike the Slickrock Trail or Practice Loop in winter.

To access the Sand Flats area from downtown Moab, go east from U.S. 191 at any of the following streets: 100 North, Center Street, 100 South or 300 South. At their intersections with 400 East, continue south to the Mill Creek Drive (by the famous Dave's Corner Market). Proceed east to the Y intersection of Mill Creek Drive and Sand Flats Road. Continue straight after the stop sign, continuing up the hill past the cemetery and recycling center 1.7 miles to the Sand Flats entrance booth. Entrance and campground fees are collected at the booth. Water is not available at the campground. Dogs are allowed on the trails but must be under control and not harassing wildlife or people. In the campground, dogs must be leashed.

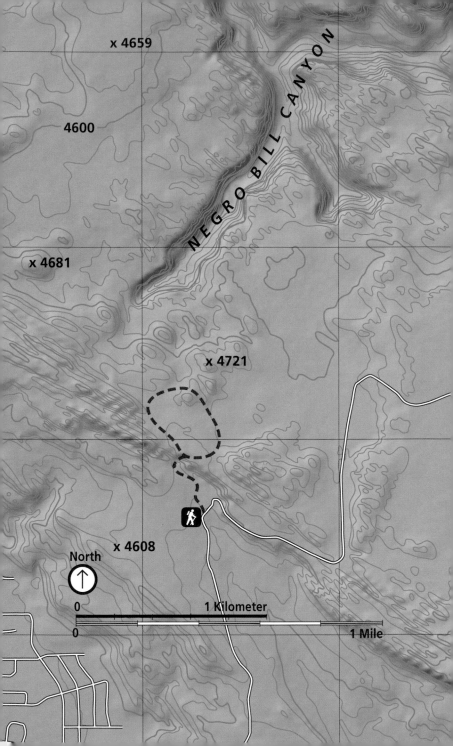

x 4659

4600

NEGRO BILL CANYON

x 4681

x 4721

x 4608

North

↑

0

1 Kilometer

0

1 Mile

IO Slickrock Bike Trail—Practice Loop

Trailhead: 0.7 miles from the entrance station.
Mileage: 2.3 miles round-trip.
Difficulty: Moderate.

This is a spectacular trail that winds across a sea of slickrock domes.
White dots mark the practice loop that intersects with the main trail.
This trail loops across a sea of Navajo Sandstone, and though it is a fun
bike ride, it also makes for an interesting walking route. Yield to mountain bikers.

Below the trail is Negro Bill Canyon, a BLM-managed Wilderness Study
Area. There is a canyon overlook at Echo Point about 0.9 miles along the
trail.

SLICKROCK

The Slickrock Trail,
pioneered by Dick
Wilson back in 1969,
along with the help of
the BLM, was origi-
nally a motorcycle
trail. Upon his return,
some thirty years later,
Wilson, dubbed "Mr.
Slickrock" by a local
Moab businessman,
could never have
guessed at the success of this trail. Although still open to motorcyclists,
this trail has been adopted worldwide by the mountain biking community. Over 100,000 riders a year take to this trail, mostly in spring and fall.
During summer, anyone riding or hiking this trail should do so in the
cooler early morning hours.

The Practice Loop is not noted for its wildlife viewing because of the
bike traffic in the area. However, occasional ravens or red-tailed hawks
are observed soaring over the trail, and a search for tracks along the
sandy washes will reveal an abundance of kangaroo rats, mice, and
woodrats. Active at night, these rodents search the sand dunes and
sparse vegetation for seeds, nuts or leaves.

II Fins & Things 4X4 Trail—Radio Tower Loop

Trailhead: Two possible starting points: the turnoff on the Sand Flats Road, 2.0 miles from the entrance station, or near the radio tower, 2.4 miles from the entrance station. The brown carsonite signs and white dinosaurs painted on the slickrock mark this trail.

Mileage: 2.5 mile round-trip.

Difficulty: Moderate.

This shared-use trail bears hiker, biker and jeeper use: it can be a nice hike. Many locals walk this loop in the off-season, when vehicle traffic is scarce. There are several short spurs that lead to overlooks of Negro Bill Canyon. Be sure to follow the signs for this loop and not the Porcupine Jeep Trail. That trail goes east of the radio towers.

The four-wheel-drive road, which is the trail, passes through sandy grasslands, climbs over slickrock fins, and provides views of the La Sal Mountains and Negro Bill Canyon. Numerous pinyon pines and Utah junipers dot the trail, although the pinyons have been dying off in recent years due to drought and the resulting invasion of the Ips beetle.

Coyotes, song dogs of the southwest, frequent the area. Their yipping and howling may be heard throughout the year. Though coyotes are carnivores, they will eat just about anything, from berries to leaves to carrion to insects to rodents. Seasonal fluctuations in their diet result from changes in prey density and food availability.

SAND FLATS AREA

Though many of the coyote's smaller prey may temporarily benefit from food leftovers found in the campground, they can become nuisance animals dependent upon these scraps. In addition, an abundance of rodents tends to attract predators other than the coyote, such as gopher snakes or rattlesnakes.

One of the more common rodents along the trail is the Ord's kangaroo rat. With massive hind feet, these rodents hop about like their marsupial namesakes. The large hind feet enable the kangaroo rat to leap from prey, but also to engage in territorial kickboxing disputes. These animals forage at night, and their tracks are visible in sandy areas.

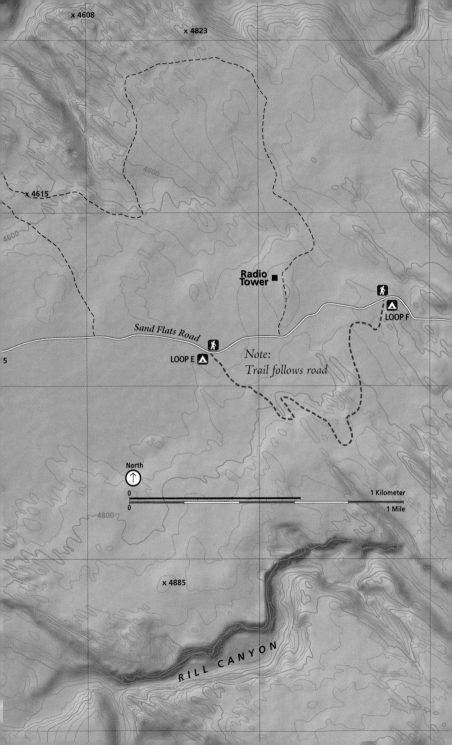

x 4608

x 4823

x 4615

4600

4600

Radio Tower ■

LOOP F 🏕

Sand Flats Road

LOOP E 🏕

Note:
Trail follows road

5

North
⬆

0
0

1 Kilometer
1 Mile

4800

x 4885

RILL CANYON

12 Fins & Things 4X4 Trail—Loop E-F

Trailhead: Turnoff from the main road at Campground Loop E (2.0 miles) and Loop F (2.4 miles) from the entrance station.
Mileage: 3.0 miles round-trip.
Difficulty: Moderate.

The trail starts to the right of campsite #5 in E Loop. Though this trail follows a four-wheel-drive road, it is a good trail to walk from the campsites. The trail climbs up the backs of Navajo Sandstone fins and across sandy flats with great views of the La Sal Mountains, Rill Canyon and far-off mesas. Hikers may encounter jeeps or mountain bikes, although you might also have the trail to yourself. If you do encounter vehicles, give them a wide berth as some of the rock climbs have sandy or loose gravel approaches.

FINS & THINGS TRAIL

The trail markers are white dinosaurs painted on either the sandstone or the signs.

Numerous pinyon pines grow along this trail. Seemingly sprouting straight from the sandstone, the short, two-needled pines produce a cyclical abundance of seeds that attract several species of birds and rodents. Flocks of dark blue pinyon jays descend upon the trees to feed, their raucous calls keeping open the lines of communication. Both the pinyon and scrub jays consume the seeds and will transport seeds to caches for later consumption in winter. Of course, some caches go untapped, and these seeds may germinate to start new seedlings.

Also present in large numbers along this trail are narrow-leaf yuccas. The bayonet-like leaves surround a long stalk that bears creamy-white flowers in spring. At night, take a flashlight and illuminate the flowers.

x 5441

PORCUPINE RIM

Note:
Trail follows road

Sand Flats Road

North

0
0   1 Kilometer
                                                    1 Mile

7000

7035

13 Porcupine Rim to Castle Valley Overlook

Trailhead: 6.5 miles from the entrance station on the Sand Flats Road.
Mileage: 4.0 miles round-trip.
Difficulty: Moderate.

UTAH JUNIPER
Juniperus osteosperma

UTAH JUNIPER & PINYON PINE
Juniperus osteosperma and Pinus edulis

From the small parking area, follow the two-track from the trailhead to an overlook of Castle Valley. This trail gains 900 feet in elevation, from 5,900 to 6,800 feet. This shared-use trail is a very popular, although difficult, mountain bike ride. Riders go from the trailhead to Utah 128, 14.4 miles away. The first 11.2 miles are open to ATV and four-wheel-drive vehicles; however, these vehicles must turn around where the two-track changes into a single track.

The hike to the overlook passes through a pinyon/juniper woodland. Early settlers noted the abundance of porcupines in the area, hence, the name Porcupine Rim. Porcupines climb the pinyon trees and gnaw off the outer bark to access the edible inner bark. Many trees bear porcupine scars—patches of missing bark on the trunk or limbs. The trees ooze a sticky sap to heal these wounds, but if the porcupine girdles the trunk, the tree will die.

Several features visible from the overlook are Round Mountain, Castle Rock (also called Castleton Tower), and Parriott Mesa. Round Mountain, located in the upper end of Castle Valley, is a volcanic plug exposed by erosion. Castle Rock is the thin spire of Wingate Sandstone that stands between the divide of Castle Valley and Professor Valley. Castle Rock is one of the classic desert climbs. Some call this Chevy Rock, named after the Chevrolet truck that was airlifted onto this spire for a television commercial. Parriott Mesa is to the west of Castle Rock. The Nature Conservancy of Utah owns the majority of this mesa, protecting the relic plant community that exists atop this mesa. These relic communities offer a rare sample of an area that has not been impacted by livestock.

Colorado River

Locally known as "The River Road," this road is worth the drive even if you don't plan on hiking. This busy road carries a mix of recreational and commuter traffic, as visitors and locals access the canyons, campgrounds and town. For a majority of its forty miles, the River Road parallels the Colorado River. Numerous pullouts provide safe vantage points from which to marvel at the river and canyon scenery. Along this road there are BLM campgrounds and private resorts.

Along the River Road you might recognize some of the steep-walled towers and spires from feature films, television, or print advertisements. Numerous movies, from John Ford westerns (*Wagon Master, Rio Grande, Cheyenne Autumn*), to *City Slickers II: The Search for Curly's Gold, Geronimo*, and *Chill Factor* have been filmed in this area. See *Where God Put the West* by Bette Stanton for more movie-making history in the Moab area.

In season, river runners ply their crafts down the "Daily" section of the Colorado River. This day-trip segment, from Hittle Bottom to the BLM Takeout, is about eighteen river miles long and consists of flatwater stretches punctuated by whitewater rapids.

x 4402

Colorado River

x 4888

x 4842

128

x 4655

x 4690

North

1 Kilometer

0

1 Mile

x 4621

NEGRO

x 4550

BILL

x 4659

CANYON

x 4618

x 4579

Morning
Glory
Natural
Bridge

x 4622

14 Negro Bill Canyon

Trailhead: Along Utah 128, 3.0 miles from the junction with U.S. Highway 191.
Mileage: 4.0 miles round-trip to Morning Glory Bridge.
Difficulty: Moderate.

Located within the BLM's Negro Bill Canyon Wilderness Study Area, this popular hike follows the canyon bottom and crosses the perennial creek multiple times. Lush riparian vegetation of Fremont cottonwood (*Populus fremontii*), Gambel's oak (*Quercus gambelii*), water birch (*Betula occidentalis*), and coyote willow (*Salix exigua*) grows along the streambanks. Crayfish scuttle through the clear pools and beavers haul tree limbs to dam the creek flow. In spring and summer, cliff swallows build their mud nests beneath protective ledges high up on the Navajo Sandstone cliffs.

When settlers returned to the Moab Valley in 1877, they met an African-American prospector named William Granstaff (Negro Bill) and Frenchie (a French-Canadian trapper) living in the abandoned Elk Mountain Mission fort. Each had laid claim to half of the fort and of the valley as well.

Negro Bill ran cattle in the canyon that bears his name and, supposedly, built a cabin up in the canyon. Some say he was an outlaw, others say he was a rancher and prospector. His departure from the county occurred after the Pinhook Battle of 1881. Accused of selling whiskey to the "renegade" Indians that were involved in that fight, Granstaff decided a change of place was in order. Fearing for his life, Granstaff moved to Colorado where he died in 1901.

To reach Morning Glory Natural Bridge, walk the trail roughly 2.0 miles to a side-canyon on the right (west) side of the canyon. Follow this side canyon 1 1/2 miles to the natural bridge. With a span of 243 feet, this bridge is in the U.S. Top 10 for longest natural rock spans. The name refers to the glorious light that bathes the arch during sunrise, not the presence of morning glory vines.

Note: Beware of poison ivy growing along the trail.

Hikers may continue upstream of this side-canyon, but the creek crossings become more challenging. Crayfish, though not native to the Colorado River and its tributaries, are abundant in this canyon. River otters and great blue herons prey upon these "mini lobsters."

Note: Because of the perennial stream, a number of hikers take their dogs on this trail. Please remember to "scoop the poop," keep a leash accessible, and be mindful of others who may not like your shaking wet dog.

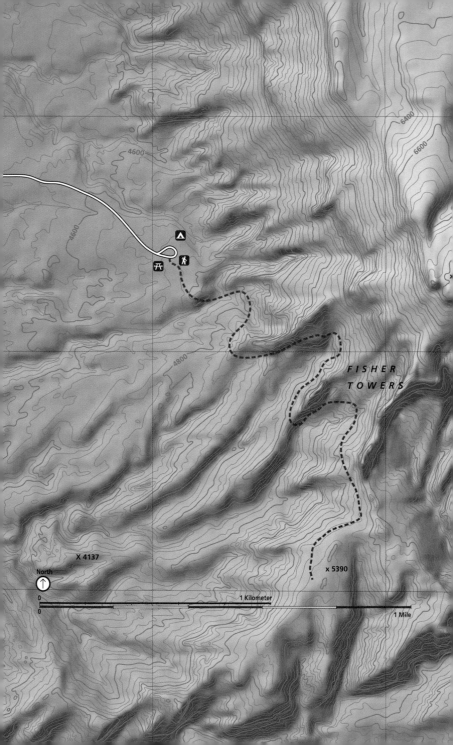

FISHER
TOWERS

X 4137

x 5390

North

0
0

1 Kilometer
1 Mile

15 Fisher Towers

Trailhead: 21 miles from the Utah 128/US 191 junction, turn onto an improved dirt road which ends at the trailhead in 2.2 miles.

Mileage: 4.4 miles round-trip.

Difficulty: Moderate.

The trail follows a sinuous path in and around large, burgundy-colored Fisher Towers and the Titan to an overlook of Onion Creek. The narrow trail drops down into the upper reaches of several side canyons of Onion Creek, loops out to unfenced overlooks, and follows level benches of sandstone where possible. Comprised of Organ Rock Shale and capped with Moenkopi Sandstone, these fantastic towers seem straight out of a child's fairytale book.

TRAIL SIGN TO FISHER TOWERS

Many rock climbing routes exist on the Titan, Fisher Towers and some of the smaller towers in this vicinity. First climbed in 1962 by Layton Kor, the Titan is over 900 feet tall; it is the tallest sandstone spire in the world.

The area takes its name from Avill and Gull Fisher, early settlers and cattlemen who resided near the mouth of Fisher Creek. Some stories say that the towers were once called Fissure Towers, named after a fissure or narrow canyon farther up the road.

The spectacular spires, canyons and mesas to the east of Fisher Towers include Professor Valley, Mary Jane Canyon, Parriott Mesa, the Priest and Nuns, Adobe Mesa, and Castle Rock. Back in the 1950s, this scenery formed the backdrop for several John Ford westerns and has provided backdrop scenery in contemporary film work such as *Geronimo*, *Canyonlands: The Living Edens*, and *Nurse Betty*.

Late afternoon lighting creates spectacular photographic opportunities at Fisher Towers, but also may make this a hot afternoon hike. A classic photo-op exists upstream of Fisher Towers along Utah 128 at milepost 24. UDOT created a paved pullout to keep visitors from stopping in the middle of the road!

x 5217

x 5242

5200

x 5191

x 4210

128

x 4098

x 4345

Colorado River

HITTLE
BOTTOM

x 4383

4200

16 Amphitheater Loop

Trailhead: Hittle Bottom Campground, near site 11.
Mileage: 2.7 miles round-trip.
Difficulty: Moderate — be careful crossing Utah 128.

This new trail, constructed in 2004, crosses Utah 128 from the Hittle Bottom Campground and creates a loop through the Richardson Amphitheater. The trail crosses different habitat types within the amphitheater. The drier uplands are dominated by blackbrush, Utah junipers, and grasses, and contrast with the riparian area along the intermittent washes. These washes have water only after heavy rainstorms or from melting snow. Rabbitbrush (*Chyrsothamnus nauseous*) is one shrub that grows along these wash bottoms. In late summer, the plant bears many yellow flowers. Native Americans did, and still do today, collect rabbitbrush flowers to use in the wool dying process. The flowers produce a beautiful golden dye.

The amphitheater is named after a professor Dr. Sylvester Richardson,

MOUNTAIN LION

who, with his wife Mary Jane, settled at the mouth of Professor Creek. A post office was established in 1886 at the store the professor built and operated. He provided supplies to the prospectors, farmers and ranchers in the area, which were brought in by boat. Richardson was one of the first county commissioners of Grand County in 1884. In 1896 Richardson ran for the office of county prosecutor. In his October 30, 1896 letter to the *Grand Valley Times* editor he writes, "I am still a candidate for County and Prosecuting Attorney. If elected will use all my salary for myself and deputy and will earn it too." Words spoken like a true politician.

Though Moab's uranium industry is often discussed after WWII, exploration and mining were active around the turn of the century. In the June 23, 1905 edition of the *Grand Valley Times* an article indicates this activity. "Whitman Cross in charge of the Government Geological Survey of the San Juan Mountain district of Colorado reached Moab...They will go up river as far as Richardson and examine the uranium properties there…"

Viewed from above, the contours of the high cliff walls form a natural amphitheater, hence, the area's name. The campground and picnic area are named after the Hittle family, who took over the Kitsen homestead at what is now known as Hittle Bottom. There is a picnic area, campground and boat launch at this site. Tom Kitsen's mother, who drowned at Hittle Bottom, is buried in the gravesite near the highway.

Heading north of Moab on U.S. 191, the Lower Courthouse Wash trailhead is on the north side of the highway, just past the Courthouse Wash Bridge. To access the Mill Canyon hike, continue north to mile marker 141.

Just past the entrance to Arches National Park, there existed an outcrop of limestone that earlier travelers had to skirt around. This jump was blasted away during construction of the old highway. The old highway alignment roughly follows the Old Spanish Trail out of Moab Canyon.

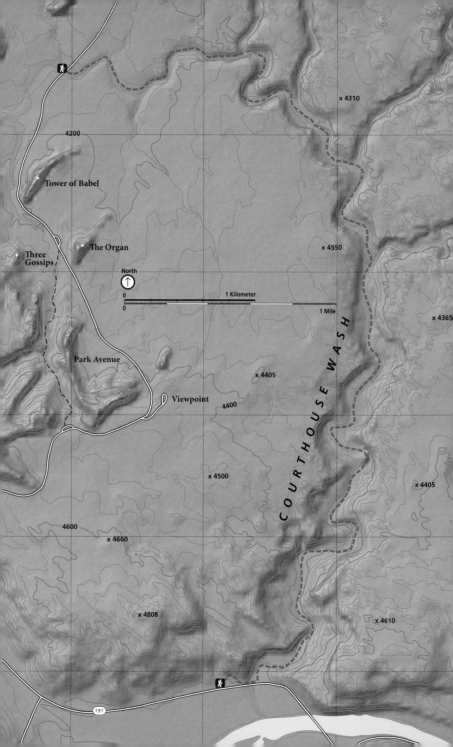

x 4310

4200

Tower of Babel

The Organ

x 4550

Three
Gossips

North
↑

0

1 Kilometer

0

1 Mile

x 4365

Park Avenue

x 4405

Viewpoint

4400

x 4500

x 4405

C O U R T H O U S E   W A S H

4600

x 4660

x 4808

x 4610

191

17 Lower Courthouse Wash – Arches National Park

Trailhead: Highway 191, 0.5 miles north of the Colorado River Bridge to the parking area on the west side of Courthouse Wash.

Mileage: 4.0 miles one-way to the Courthouse Wash Bridge in Arches National Park.

Difficulty: Moderate.

Follow the trail from the parking area across the Courthouse Wash Bridge. A short spur trail at the mouth of the canyon leads to a large pictograph panel on the south wall. This panel is visible from the main trail with binoculars.

The main trail continues upstream on the east side of Courthouse Wash and crosses a fence line (please close the gate). You can either follow the creek or the trails along the wash bottoms. Expect to get your feet wet, especially in the lower end. During spring runoff, the Colorado River might back up into the wash, sometimes to the point that you have to wade across the water. Proceed upstream; it is 4.0 miles to the Courthouse Wash Bridge in the park.

Courthouse Wash is deeply entrenched in this lower portion of the canyon. Bordered by high Navajo Sandstone walls, there are several side canyons in this lower end worth exploring.

Groves of cottonwoods find rootholds along most of Courthouse Wash. Able to withstand periodic flooding, these trees release copious amounts of seeds in late spring and early summer, earning this time period the nickname "Snow in Summer." The seed release coincides with the declining flood stage of the river. Fresh sediments deposited by the runoff provide ideal germination sites for the cottonwood seeds, and the seedlings' roots grow quickly in the moist soil.

Cooper's hawks, small raptors with a call that sounds like a maniac's laugh, build their stick nests high up in these cottonwoods. These predators hunt birds, mammals, even lizards, and have been known to dive-bomb intruders that are too close to their nest sites. There are several historic nesting territories along this lower portion of the wash.

Note: A shuttle may be arranged by parking vehicles at the Lower Courthouse Wash parking area and at the Courthouse Wash Bridge in Arches National Park.

One wildlife species that appears in June and July in the canyon is the deer fly. The larvae live in the wash bottom's saturated sand. Their jaws project just above the sandy surface and grab aquatic insects and tadpoles for food. The adults emerge in June and they are voracious biters. Swarms of these flies have driven many an unprepared hiker from the wash. Since they seem to mainly bite the lower extremities, wearing lightweight hiking pants and a long-sleeved shirt reduces the square footage of available flesh.

This wash dries up in the summer except when flash floods come rumbling down the canyon. The Courthouse Wash/Seven Mile Canyon complex encompasses a vast runoff area, so rainstorms far upstream may result in a flood even in what starts as a dry portion of the canyon.

These trails might fall into the category of strolls rather than hikes. Designed for either the after-dinner crowd or the in-town walker, the trails provide a fun alternative to your Moab experience. These trails provides an excellent way to access downtown areas without having to walk or ride a bike along the streets.

Through easements, donations, state funding, and direct land purchases, the City of Moab created the Mill Creek Parkway. Dedicated on June 4, 1999, the Mill Creek Parkway offers a walking/biking

opportunity along Mill and Pack creeks through town. There are short spur trails along Pack Creek, one to the west of the Grand County High School and another through Bullock's Marsh (Cross Creeks Park) just west of 200 South.

There are numerous access points to this parkway trail. There are areas to park your car at Rotary Park along Mill Creek Drive, on 100 E. and 300 S., and by the Grand County School Bus Barn on 400 East.

x 4721

191

x 4608

100 South

Mill Creek

Rotary
Park

Sand Flats Rd.

400 East

x 4087

Mill Creek

x 4159

Pack Creek

191

x 5228

North
↑

0   1 Kilometer

0   1 Mile

x 5305

18   Mill Creek Parkway – Rotary Park to Main Street

Trailhead: Rotary Park on Mill Creek Drive.
Mileage: 1.0 mile one-way.
Difficulty: Easy.

From Rotary Park, the trail follows the course of Mill Creek, a main drainage of the La Sal Mountains. Many Moab residents walk their dogs (on leash in City limits), take a leisurely afternoon stroll, bike to home or work, in-line skate or jog for exercise, or bird watch along this trail. Mule deer, striped skunk, gray fox, rock squirrels, western garter snakes, and bullfrogs are just some of the non-feathered wildlife one may encounter along the trail. Providing an "off-road" experience and glimpse of the riparian corridor through a portion of town, the trail is limited to non-motorized use.

The Canyon Country Museum of Moab, formerly the Dan O'Laurie Canyon Country Museum, has donated historical farming equipment for an outdoor exhibit that is located between Rotary Park and 400 East. At Rotary Park there are swing sets, tree forts, picnic tables, and some musical instruments called gamelins for entertainment.

WOOD DUCK

For bird watchers, the best section of trail is from 400 East to 300 South. Here you might encounter western screech owls, wood ducks, white-breasted nuthatches, yellow-rumped warblers, or cedar waxwings. Take the alternate wood chip strewn path down to the creek for better birding.

COOPER'S HAWK

x 4681

191

No Parking

500 West

100 South

Kane Creek

Mill Creek

x 4087

400 East

x 5228

North

↑

0

1 Kilometer

0

1 Mile

191

19 Mill Creek Parkway – Main Street to 500 West

Trailhead: The primary access points for this trail are just west of the Gonzo Inn and 500 West.
Mileage: 1.2 miles one-way, includes Bullock's Marsh Loop.
Difficulty: Easy.

The Canyon Country Museum of Moab has set up historical mining equipment at the footbridge across Mill Creek, just west of the Gonzo Inn. Proceeding downstream from this area leads one to 500 West. The City of Moab has purchased a section of property west of the 500 West Bridge and is working to obtain easements to the Scott M. Matheson Wetlands Preserve. When that trail is complete, it may be possible to access this trail from the preserve's parking lot on Kane Creek Boulevard.

There is a small loop, downstream of the Gonzo Inn that winds through

EVENING GROSBEAK

Bullock's Marsh and returns to 200 South. This is a good birdwatching area, with Bullock's orioles, black-headed grosbeaks, and yellow-rumped warblers. The burned out trees are a stark reminder of the power of fire. This trail is at times overgrown with vegetation; stick to the main trail and cross the small footbridges across Pack Creek to return to the paved road.

The junction of Pack and Mill Creeks is not visible along the trail. Pack Creek received its name from packs cached near the creek by the William D. Huntington and Jackson Stewart trading-exploration expedition in 1854.

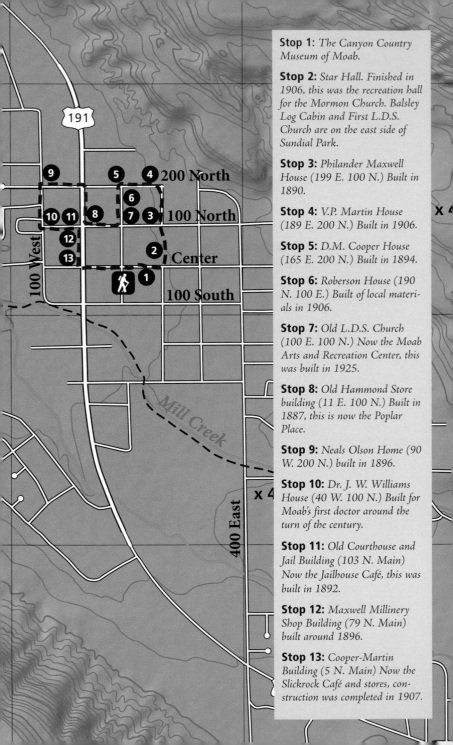

Stop 1: *The Canyon Country Museum of Moab.*

Stop 2: *Star Hall. Finished in 1906, this was the recreation hall for the Mormon Church. Balsley Log Cabin and First L.D.S. Church are on the east side of Sundial Park.*

Stop 3: *Philander Maxwell House (199 E. 100 N.) Built in 1890.*

Stop 4: *V.P. Martin House (189 E. 200 N.) Built in 1906.*

Stop 5: *D.M. Cooper House (165 E. 200 N.) Built in 1894.*

Stop 6: *Roberson House (190 N. 100 E.) Built of local materials in 1906.*

Stop 7: *Old L.D.S. Church (100 E. 100 N.) Now the Moab Arts and Recreation Center, this was built in 1925.*

Stop 8: *Old Hammond Store building (11 E. 100 N.) Built in 1887, this is now the Poplar Place.*

Stop 9: *Neals Olson Home (90 W. 200 N.) built in 1896.*

Stop 10: *Dr. J. W. Williams House (40 W. 100 N.) Built for Moab's first doctor around the turn of the century.*

Stop 11: *Old Courthouse and Jail Building (103 N. Main) Now the Jailhouse Café, this was built in 1892.*

Stop 12: *Maxwell Millinery Shop Building (79 N. Main) built around 1896.*

Stop 13: *Cooper-Martin Building (5 N. Main) Now the Slickrock Café and stores, construction was completed in 1907.*

Historic Walking Tour

Trailhead: Start at the Moab Information Center (MIC) located at Center and Main.
Mileage: 0.75 mile round-trip.
Difficulty: Easy.

This twelve block walking tour of the Old Town District of Moab passes by several historic homes and buildings. There is a brochure, available at the Moab Information Center or The Canyon Country Museum of Moab that provides a glimpse into the past occupants and businesses that resided in these buildings. The Canyon Country Museum of Moab is along this walk. The museum provides interesting displays, temporary exhibits and additional information about the area's history. Hours vary.

A suggested route is shown on the map. This differs from the museum's brochure, since the Balsley Log Cabin was moved. This walk makes for an interesting and easy evening stroll. Your route could also be based upon your accommodation, shopping or dining choices. Some of the historical houses are private residences. Please do not disturb the owners.

MAXWELL HOUSE HOTEL, 1886

STAR HALL, 1909

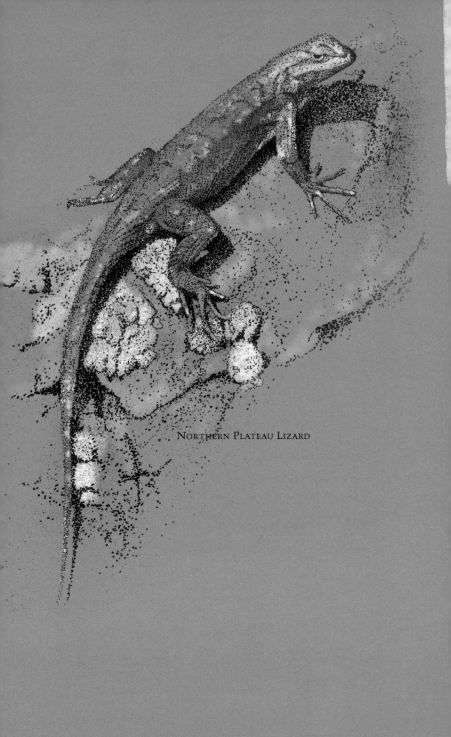

Northern Plateau Lizard

This section is south and west of U.S. Highway 191. The only trail in this section is Hidden Valley, which starts on the edge of a residential area. There are numerous mountain biking and four-wheel-drive roads in the Behind-the-Rocks area, but there are not any well-marked or maintained trails in this area. Located in a proposed Wilderness Study Area, there are many off-trail hiking areas in this sandstone wilderness.

ad: 3.0 miles south of the intersection of U.S. Highway 191 and Kane Creek ...evard, turn west (right) onto Angel Rock Road. Continue to the intersection with ...nrock Road and turn north (right) onto Rimrock Road. The trailhead parking area is ...bout 0.5 miles down this dirt road. Weather conditions may affect the condition of the improved dirt road section along Rimrock Road.

Mileage: 4.0 miles round-trip, 2.0 miles to connecting Moab Rim Trail.

Difficulty: Moderate to Difficult.

The trail to Hidden Valley switchbacks up a steep talus slope until it reaches a "hidden valley"—a broad shelf that is blocked by rock formations—to the east. Hidden from the scrutiny of Spanish Valley, the trail levels out and passes through this valley to connect to the Moab Rim Trail. High Wingate Sandstone cliffs form the eastern escarpment of the Behind-the-Rocks area and create a dramatic backdrop to the valley below.

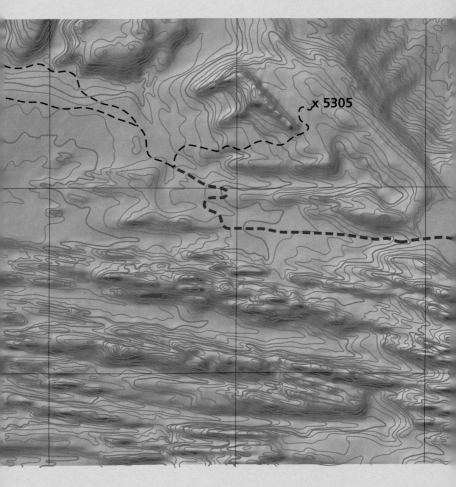

Golden eagles build huge stick nests on protective ledges within this escarpment. Protected from intruders or predators, these "booted eagles" (meaning their legs are feathered to their toes) patrol the skies above the Moab Valley in search of prey. Cottontails, jackrabbits, chukars, and carrion are some of the prey items that the eagles feed on.

The trail was originally part of a route the Native Americans used to access the area above Spanish Valley. Scattered rock art sites exist, with one visible where the trail connects to the Moab Rim Trail.

Mountain bikers may use this trail as well, although many end up carrying their bikes down the switchbacks. Yield to bikers by stepping to the side of the trail.

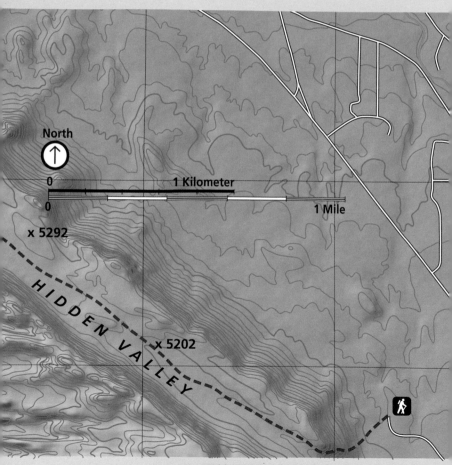

Dedicated June 5, 1981, Ken's Lake is a man-made reservoir fed by a diversion from Mill Creek. Designed for agricultural irrigation in Spanish Valley, the lake is named after a former Moab mayor and water conservancy district chairman, Ken McDougald, for his long-standing support of civic projects. Ken's Lake holds an estimated 2,750 acre-feet of water when full. The dam is 96 feet high and 4,050 feet long, with a maximum lake depth of 70 feet.

Water from Mill Creek is diverted through the Sheley Tunnel, a 645-foot-long tunnel named after Horace Sheley. Sheley had attempted to divert water from Mill Creek around the turn of the century, but never completed the project. The waterfall

at the base of the cliff is accessible by the Faux Falls Trail from the campground. BLM operates a 31-site campground and day use area near the shore of Ken's Lake.

Though the water level in the lake fluctuates, there always seem to be some recreationists at the lake, fishing, swimming, wind surfing, or working on their kayak rolls. Motors are not allowed on the lake.

The trails in this area may be accessed from the campground or from the beach parking area for day users.

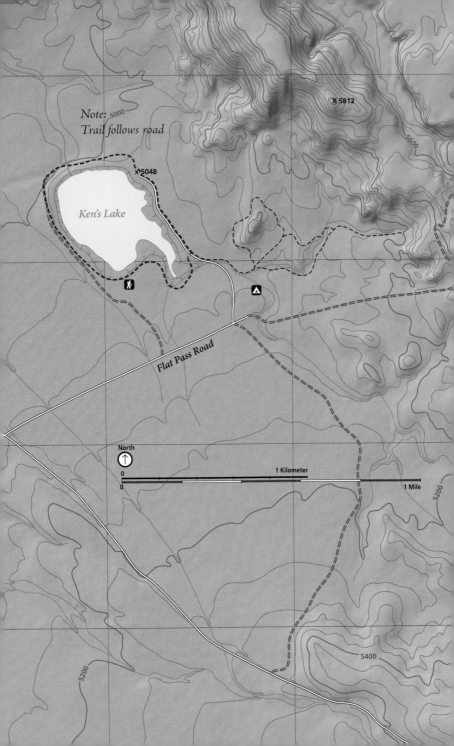

Note:
Trail follows road

X 5812

X 5048

Ken's Lake

Flat Pass Road

North
↑

0
0

1 Kilometer

1 Mile

5000

5600

5200

5200

5400

Trailhead: Ken's Lake Campground between sites 12 and 14.
Mileage: 1.9 miles round-trip.
Difficulty: Easy.

This trailhead starts between campsites 12 and 14. The trail follows the edge of the lake across the dikes and back to the campground by crossing the lake's inlet near site 18.

Though not a "wilderness" hike by any means, this easy walking trail provides access to the lake and views of Spanish Valley and the La Sal Mountains. At times there may be a lot of local traffic at the lake—people swimming, fishing, or hanging out. The Utah Division of Wildlife Resources stocks the lake with catchable-size brown and rainbow trout, sunfish, large-mouthed bass, and channel catfish, but don't forget your fishing license.

PRICKLY PEAR CACTUS
Opuntia erinacea

Migrating ospreys, ducks or loons may be observed feeding or loafing on the lake. The most common bird around the lake is the horned lark, named for the male's two dark horn-like feathers. These birds nest on the ground and prefer close-cropped vegetation.

On the east side of the lake there are numerous pinyon trees that attract pinyon jays in the fall. These birds harvest the pinyon nuts, caching some for winter consumption. Though it may seem haphazard where the birds deposit seeds, their memories serve them well. In fact, the birds scored better than a flock of graduate students in a study designed to test cache relocating abilities. Noisy flocks of the dark blue jays descend upon the trees when the cones open to reveal the nuts. Able to distinguish ripe seeds from infertile ones through color and weight, the jays are amazing to watch harvesting this bounty.

Where the trail crosses the small inlet creek back to the campground, there is a different assemblage of vegetation than in the uplands around the lake. Cottonwoods and willows line the inlet, and in turn, attract different birds than the coniferous forests of pinyon and juniper. Look for warblers, vireos and orioles searching for insects in the riparian vegetation, as well as American dippers exploring for insects beneath the water.

X 5812

5000

5048

Ken's Lake

Flat Pass Road

North

0

1 Kilometer

1 Mile

5600

5200

5400

5200

23 Faux Falls Trail

Trailhead: Ken's Lake Campground between sites 18 and 19.
Mileage: 1.6 miles round-trip.
Difficulty: Moderate.

SHORT-HORNED LIZARD

CLIFF-ROSE
Purshia mexicana

This trail follows a four-wheel-drive-road, which connects to the campground exit and follows the creek to the falls on the south side of the inlet stream. The return loop is on the north side of this inlet.

The false or "faux" waterfall provides an interesting contrast in this land of rock and sand. The water cascades down the cliff slope from the diversion point beneath the Flat Pass Road. The diversion began in 1981 and it is amazing to see cottonwoods and willows getting established along this watercourse.

At the falls there are rock steps for crossing the inlet and continuing on the loop back to the campground. Like many hikes in the Moab area, this one also features the plants and animals of the pinyon-juniper woodlands. In late spring the large cliffrose shrubs may be cloaked with blossoms and, in turn, are swarmed with insects seeking sweet nectar. These shrubs may have a second bloom period later in late summer if conditions are right.

Along this return trail and portions of the Rock Trail, you might notice some different looking rocks. There are numerous granite cobbles and boulders mixed in with the sandstone ones. These rocks are from the La Sal Mountains washed down thousands of years ago in Mill Creek floods.

Eventually the narrow path connects to an old road. This is the junction with the Rock Trail loop. You can either proceed downstream along the creek or head up the road and loop back on the Rock Trail. Either trail will eventually lead back to the campground.

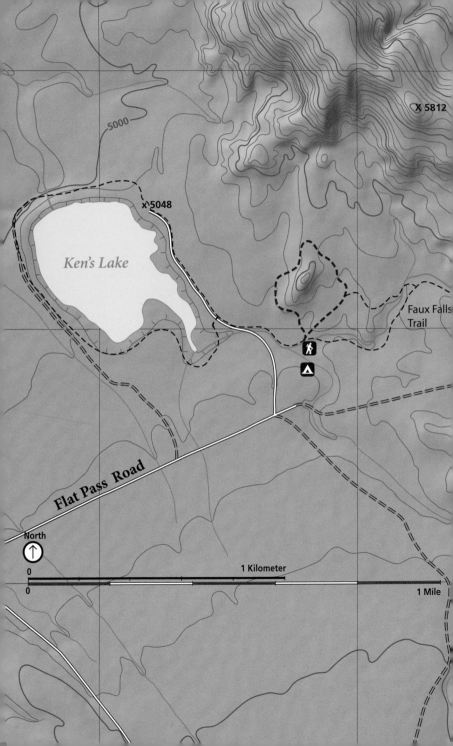

X 5812

−5000−

x 5048

Ken's Lake

Faux Falls
Trail

Flat Pass Road

North
↑

0
1 Kilometer
0
1 Mile

24 Rock Trail

Trailhead: Ken's Lake Campground between sites 18 and 19.
Mileage: 0.8 mile round-trip.
Difficulty: Moderate.

This trail circles the large outcrop of Navajo Sandstone called The Rock on the east side of the lake. There is a steep ascent on the northern portion of this trail, but it is not difficult. Since this is a fairly new trail, be aware of the cairns that mark the trail, as the path is not very evident. Portions of this trail follow an old road, then hook up with an equestrian trail from the north.

INDIAN PAINTBRUSH
Castilleja chromosa

Near the west side of The Rock there are some different cobbles and boulders. These rocks are granitic in origin, not sandstone eroded from the nearby cliffs.

RED-SPOTTED TOAD
Bufo punctatus

Cheatgrass, an introduced weedy grass, named because it sprouts quickly in the early spring and thus "cheats" the competition, is pervasive in this area. An indicator of overgrazing or extensive cultivation, cheatgrass prefers disturbed areas where it can become established. Areas with extensive infestations of cheatgrass are vulnerable to summer wildfires and, since its seeds are fire adapted, will outcompete other grasses and forbs in getting established in the burned areas. The flower heads have small spines that imbed in the lips of livestock or the socks of humans.

This trail intersects with the Faux Falls Trail on the south side of The Rock. From this intersection one can either hike to the falls or return directly to the campground.

In the 1963 version of Freeman Tilden's *The National Parks*, he writes about Arches National Monument: "Not far from the old Mormon pioneer town of Moab, Utah, a great mass of buff-colored sandstone towers over the surrounding plain. Into this thick rock the weathering forces of nature have cut more natural stone arches, windows, spires, and pinnacles than are to be found anywhere else in the country. So far, eighty-eight openings large enough to be called arches have been discovered within the boundaries of this monument, but it is certain others will be found hidden away in the less accessible rugged parts of the area." Others, indeed.

Ed McCarrick, Dale Stevens and Rubin Scholnick were three of the more famous arch hunters to prowl the park. McCarrick worked for Arches National Park as a naturalist, meeting up with Stevens and Scholnick through their overlapping interests. Like detectives, the trio would follow a lead about some obscure arch, usually finding several others in the process. They established arch criteria—the span had to be a minimum of 36 inches and created within a continuous rock wall. With these criteria, this trio surpassed 2,000 named arches. Chris Moore and others took up the torch after Ed McCarrick passed away in 1992. To date, there are over 2,500 named arches in the park.

A Hungarian immigrant, Alexander Ringhoffer moved to southeastern Utah in 1917. Since he was a prospector, Ringhoffer covered much of the area in search of mineral deposits. Enraptured with the Klondike Bluffs area, he convinced Denver and Rio Grande Railroad (DRG) officials to visit the area as a possible tourist attraction. He chiseled his name at the base of Tower Arch in 1922.

Ringhoffer's efforts were echoed by J.W. "Doc" Williams and Loren "Bish" Taylor. They and others worked hard for the designation of a national monument; President Herbert Hoover signed a proclamation declaring Arches National Monument on February 25, 1929. Two sections, the Windows and Devils Garden, totaling 4,520 acres were set aside. Ironically, Delicate Arch, the icon of the park, was not included in that original designation.

Frank Beckwith, a newspaper editor from Delta, Utah, led an expedition in 1933-1934 to complete an accurate boundary and archaeological survey of the new monument. His official report, maps and articles stimulated the interest to expand the monument. Local opposition to this enlargement was vocal, although again supporters such as *Times-Independent* editor Taylor, Doc Williams, and others silenced the naysayers. In 1938, President Franklin Delano Roosevelt enlarged the monument to 33,680 acres, of which the Courthouse Towers and Delicate Arch sections were included.

At this time the Willow Springs Road was the primary access from U.S. Highway 191. Rough and rocky, this road entered the park just west of Balanced Rock. Edward Abbey wrote *Desert Solitaire*, an accounting of his seasonal park ranger days, while living in a trailer near Balanced Rock.

A new entrance road was completed in 1958. This provided paved access into the park from the Visitor Center.

During the "Uranium Frenzy" of the early 1960s, Dwight D. Eisenhower carved 720 acres from the monument's northeast corner for mineral development. In exchange, 480 acres were added.

President Lyndon B. Johnson doubled the size of the monument in 1969 by executive order. This action set the stage for the monument to become a national park in 1971. With this designation, the park again downsized to 73,233 acres.

A recent addition in the 1990s included the Lost Spring drainage of Salt Wash in the park. The addition of this remote section brought the total to 76,359 acres.

The primary rock formation in the park is the Entrada Sandstone. This contains sediments laid down during the Jurassic Period over 150 million years ago. The sediments were offshore or coastal deposits from the broad ocean that covered most of the western United States during that time. The three important layers are the Moab Member of the Curtis Formation, the Slick Rock Member of the Entrada Sandstone and the Dewey Bridge Member of the Carmel Formation.

Tower of Babel

Sheep Rock

Courthouse Towers
Viewpoint

The Organ

Three Gossips

COURTHOUSE
TOWERS

Park Avenue

La Sal
Mountain
Viewpoint

Park Avenue Viewpoint

Moab Fault Overlook

PARK HEADQUARTERS

North

0   1 Kilometer

0   1 Mile

191

25 Park Avenue

Trailhead: Two trailheads — Courthouse Towers, 3.7 miles from the Visitor Center or Park Avenue, 2.5 miles from the Visitor Center.
Mileage: 1.0 mile one-way.
Difficulty: Easy to moderate.

New York has its famed Park Avenue of glass and metal, while Arches National Park has its avenue of stone skyscrapers—without the constant honking. The monoliths of stone eroded into the canyon walls reminded early explorers of the New York cityscape; hence, the name.

The Park Avenue Trail can be hiked from either parking area. The National Park Service recommends that hikers retrace their steps to their vehicles rather than walking back to their vehicles via the road. I would recommend hiking south to north (downstream), especially if you have a shuttle driver who will meet you at the other end.

From the Park Avenue area the trail follows the cement path to the overlook, then descends into the canyon. Notice the balanced rocks on the west (left) side of the canyon. Popsicle Rock is the small, narrow tower and Queen Nefertiti is the Egyptian queen-looking rock perched on the canyon rim.

During spring, there may be over twenty-five species of plants blooming along this short trail. Indian paintbrush (*Castilleja chromosa*) is a low-growing perennial that brightens up the path in early spring with its brilliant red blossoms. The red bracts enclose green flowers; the red color attracts hummingbirds that serve as pollinators for the flowers. Another early spring flower is the Newberry's twinpod (*Physaria newberryi*), a member of the Mustard Family (Brassicaceae). The $1/4$ to $1/2$-inch yellow flowers have four petals in the shape of a cross. The seed pods resemble two fused inflated pods, hence the common name "twinpod."

At the lower end of the hike, the trail crosses a wide portion of slickrock. Runoff has eroded a series of small basins in the slickrock. Aquatic creatures, from $1/2$-inch long translucent fairy shrimp to red-spotted toads, occur in these watery universes. Because of the ephemeral nature of the pools, the inhabitants attempt to race through their life cycles before the pools dry up. Look closely for these creatures but remember not to touch or sit in the water, for this disturbs the delicate chemical balance of life that exists in these potholes.

Towers of Entrada Sandstone—the Organ and the Tower of Babel— surround the Courthouse Towers trailhead. Sheep Rock, Baby Arch, and the Three Gossips are other features visible from this trailhead. Keep an eye open for climbers ascending these towers for a perspective on the size of these monoliths.

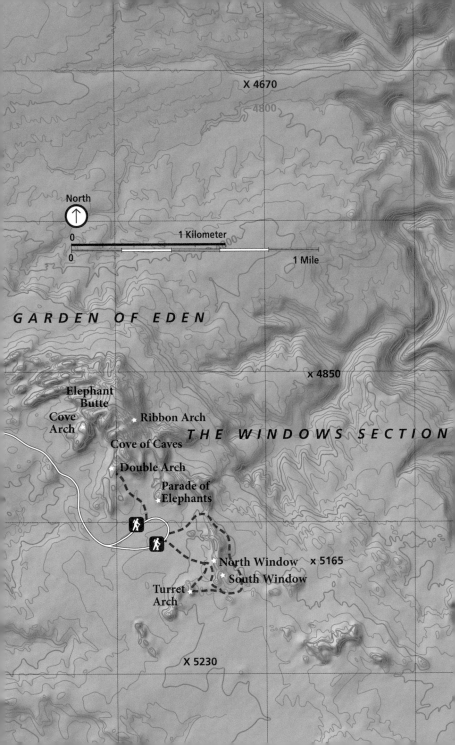

X 4670

4800

North
↑

0
1 Kilometer
0
1 Mile

GARDEN OF EDEN

Elephant
Butte
Cove
Arch
★ Ribbon Arch

Cove of Caves

THE WINDOWS SECTION

Double Arch

Parade of
Elephants

North Window x 5165
South Window

Turret
Arch

X 5230

26 The Windows

Trailhead: North and South Window Parking Area, 11.7 miles from the Visitor Center. Parking for Double Arch is just ¼ mile farther along the road.

Mileage: 1.0-mile round-trip for the Windows, 0.8 mile round-trip for Double Arch.

Difficulty: Easy.

This is a very popular hike within the park. The recently reconstructed trail loops between three massive arches: Turret Arch, and North and South Window. Together the two windows are called The Spectacles, and you'll see why when you view these windows from Turret Arch or the primitive loop trail.

Several shrubs in the Rose Family are abundant along this trail. Cliff-rose (*Purshia mexicana*) is a large shrub with small glossy, five-lobed leaves. These plants may bloom twice a year, once during spring and again later in the summer. The spring bloom is more intense as the plants may be cloaked with fragrant, creamy-white blossoms.

Blackbrush (*Coleogyne ramosissima*) is another member of the Rose Family (Rosaceae) that occurs here. This is one of the dominant shrubs growing in the park. The low-growing shrubs bear ³⁄₈-inch long narrow leaves and yellow flowers that eventually form a hard seed. Small rodents

BLACKBRUSH
Coleogyne ramosissima

harvest these seeds. Blackbrush is an important winter browse plant for mule deer or bighorn sheep since the leaves are evergreen.

From South Window, there is a primitive trail that loops behind the Windows and returns to the parking area. The entire trail is 1.0 mile long, and offers a "behind the eyes" view of these rocky spectacles.

The trail to Double Arch, just across the loop, is 0.8 miles round-trip and offers the opportunity to see a unique structure. At one time there may have been a large pothole in the sandstone that formed the roof of Double Arch. Erosion wore a hole in the bottom of this pothole and runoff from rainstorms or snowmelt cascaded through and out the sandstone wall to the south. This created the upper opening and the lower one. Additional erosion wore through the back wall, creating a third opening.

You can access the Double Arch trailhead by walking the short trail from the south end of the Windows parking area or by driving around the loop to the other parking area.

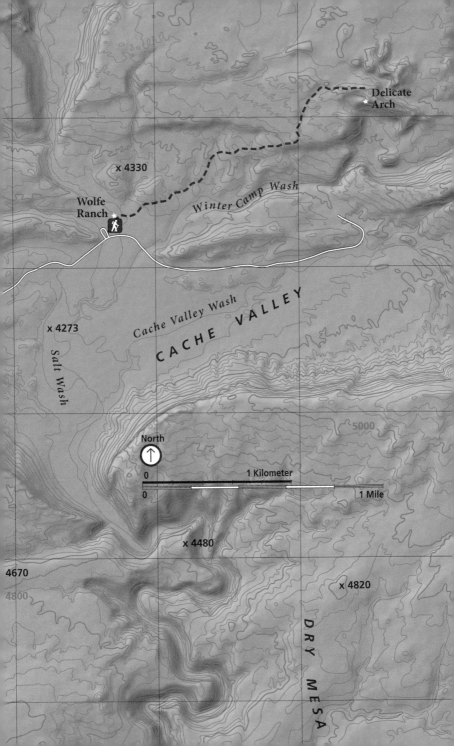

Delicate
Arch

x 4330

Wolfe
Ranch

Winter Camp Wash

Cache Valley Wash

CACHE VALLEY

x 4273

Salt Wash

5000

North

↑

0

0

1 Kilometer

1 Mile

x 4480

4670

x 4820

4800

DRY MESA

Delicate Arch

Trailhead: Delicate Arch trailhead at Wolfe Cabin, 12.9 miles from the Visitor Center.

Mileage: 3.0 miles round-trip.

Difficulty: Strenuous. Be aware of drop-offs, high winds, lightning, and wet or icy conditions.

Delicate Arch is a Utah icon found on license plates, government stationery, and in numerous advertisements. Simply put, this is one of the "must see" arches of the park, whether from this trail or the shorter Delicate Arch Viewpoint Trail.

Near the trailhead is the historic Wolfe Ranch. John Wesley Wolfe and his son Fred homesteaded this area in 1898. Wolfe, a retired Civil War veteran, moved to the desert for his health. Though this seems like a remote location today, the opportunity to homestead an area with a good supply of fresh water enticed Wolfe to stay. In addition, the railroad stop at Thompson Springs was but a day's wagon trip away. Wolfe stayed in the area until 1910.

Wolfe called his ranch the "Bar DX." He ran some cattle and grew vegetables in a garden. The original cabin was destroyed in a flash flood; the current one was built in 1906.

Just beyond the Salt Wash footbridge is a short spur trail to a Ute petroglyph panel. A sign marks the way. The figures on horseback date to post-Spanish settlement time, as horses were not in the Southwest during the Ancestral Puebloan period.

After you visit the petroglyph panel, return to the main trail. The trail climbs up and around a small ridge that contains some very colorful boulders. These boulders bear large chert nodules and are erosional remnants of the Tidwell Member of the Morrison Formation. Native Americans knapped this hard rock into spearpoints, knife blades, arrowheads, and scrapers.

Note: This is a very popular photogenic spot at sunset. Remember to bring a flashlight for the return trip.

Past these boulders the trail climbs a steep, open section of slickrock. There is a path worn into the sandstone from the feet of many hikers. Take a moment along this section to stop and look at the Windows Section on the far distance skyline.

Close to Delicate Arch, at the start of the blasted section of trail, is a small round arch. This is Frame Arch, named because photographers can "frame" Delicate Arch through this arch. If you look closely along the blasted section of trail that leads from Frame Arch to Delicate, you'll notice bore holes that were drilled in the sandstone. The blasted trail section was built to provide a safer approach to the arch; however, be careful when icy conditions exist in winter.

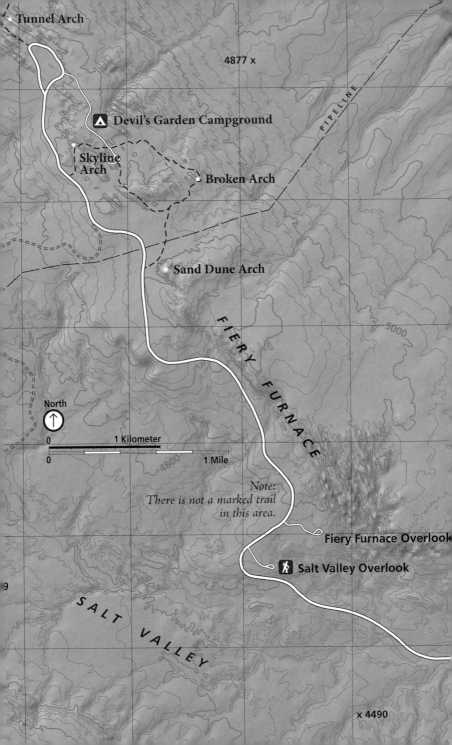

Tunnel Arch

4877 x

PIPELINE

▲ Devil's Garden Campground

Skyline Arch

Broken Arch

Sand Dune Arch

FIERY FURNACE

5000

North

↑

0
1 Kilometer

0
1 Mile

4800

Note:
*There is not a marked trail
in this area.*

Fiery Furnace Overlook

🚶 Salt Valley Overlook

SALT VALLEY

x 4490

9

28 Fiery Furnace

Trailhead: The trailhead is 14.5 miles from the Visitor Center on the main park road.
Mileage: The highly recommended guided walk is approximately 2.0 miles round-trip.
Difficulty: Moderate. Reservations accepted at www.Recreation.gov or sign up at the Visitor Center.

Named for the fire-like coloration of the Entrada Sandstone at sunrise and sunset, the Fiery Furnace is a very "cool" place. Temperatures inside the furnace are cooler due to the high, narrow fins of sandstone.

FIERY FURNACE

Park Rangers lead guided tours through this labyrinth of sandstone canyons and fins; there are no marked trails in this area. Tours average 2.5-3 hours and advanced reservations and a fee are required. Either sign up at the Visitor Center (up to 7 days in advance) or make a reservation on-line at www.Recreation.gov. Children 5 and under are not permitted on the guided walk.

Hikers wishing to enter into this area on their own need to obtain a permit available only at the Visitor Center. There is a small fee for the permit and the Park Service requires visitors to watch a short video about minimum impact practices before exploring the Fiery Furnace. The recommendation is to take the tour first so you have some idea of the route.

Along the route hikers squeeze through narrow fins of sandstone, climb up and over some small boulders, walk up slopes of slickrock, and traverse ledges with exposure and drop-offs. Children, watch your parents, and vice versa, at the unfenced sections of the trail. This is not an easy route, but it is well worth the effort. Keep your eyes open for two spectacular arches, Skull and Surprise.

In early spring, the Canyonlands biscuitroot (*Lomatium latilobum*) sends up a cluster of yellowish flowers. Visitors often note a skunk-like smell where these plants bloom. This aroma is to attract flies and other insects as pollinators. Related to carrots, this plant grows in close association with Entrada Sandstone fins, thus it has a very limited distribution in south-eastern Utah. The plants often grow on sandy mounds at the base of the fins. Please avoid walking on these mounds, as the shifting sands may expose the roots to desiccation.

Though you may not see much wildlife in here, tracks of mule deer, cottontails, small rodents, and ravens litter the sandy washes. These tracks attest to the nocturnal or early morning activity of the wildlife in the Furnace.

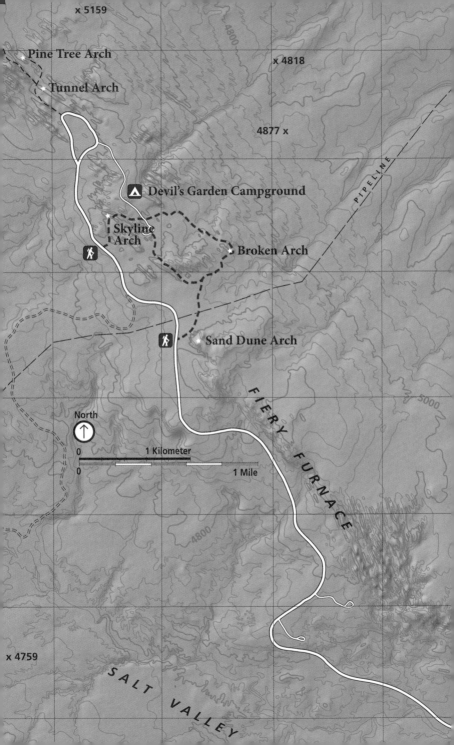

29 Sand Dune/Broken Arch

Trailhead: The trailhead is 16.5 miles from the Visitor Center on the main road. Campers may also access this trail from the campground near site #40.
Mileage: 1.2 miles round-trip.
Difficulty: Easy.

Sand Dune Arch wins the award for Kid's Favorite Arch. Located between steep Entrada Sandstone fins, Sand Dune Arch is relatively small, but has a steep sandy slope that makes it seem larger. Kids enjoy playing in this.

Another temptation here is to climb up onto the arch and jump to the sand dune below. Don't do it. There have been numerous rescues at this site, most involve back injuries from people who jumped off the arch. It is against park regulations to climb atop any named arch, but common sense should dictate that this is not a safe practice.

From Sand Dune Arch, the trail continues across the open meadow to Broken Arch. This arch sports a cap of white Moab Member of the Curtis Formation and is named for the large fracture in the top of the span.

In the vicinity of Broken Arch, kit fox, long-nosed leopard lizards, mule deer, and common ravens are a few of the wildlife species that might be observed. Kit foxes are small desert foxes with huge ears and long, bushy tails. Their black-tipped tails account for about 40% of their body length. Females excavate den sites in the stabilized sand dunes and bear a litter of pups in February or March. Mostly nocturnal, the pups may be active outside the den about a month later. Kit foxes prey on rabbits, small rodents, insects, and ground-nesting birds, lizards, and snakes.

Ravens build large stick nests in protective alcoves or cracks in the cliff wall. Their noisy young are the best way to locate a nest, as their begging calls may be heard from quite a distance.

RAVEN EGGS

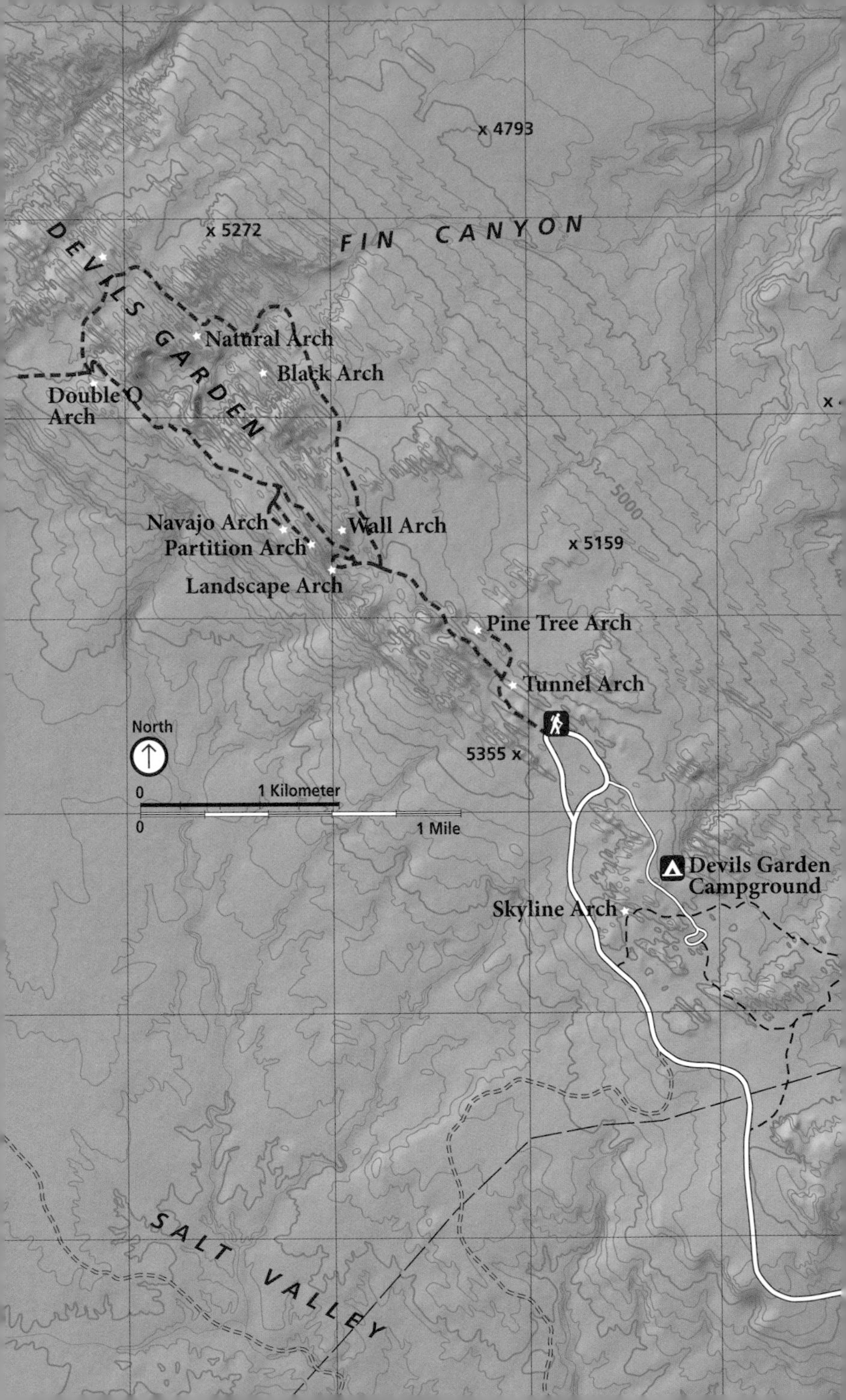

x 4793

FIN CANYON

x 5272

DEVILS GARDEN

Natural Arch

Black Arch

Double O
Arch

Navajo Arch
Partition Arch

Wall Arch

Landscape Arch

x 5159

x 5000

Pine Tree Arch

Tunnel Arch

5355 x

North
↑

0   1 Kilometer

0   1 Mile

Devils Garden
Campground

Skyline Arch

SALT VALLEY

30 Devils Garden Trail

Trailhead: 17.7 miles from the Visitor Center.

Mileage: Up to 7.2 miles round-trip.

Difficulty: Easy to difficult depending upon the length of the hike. Beyond Landscape Arch the trail crosses some exposed sections. Be aware of dropoffs, high winds and wet or icy condition.

This is the longest maintained trail in the park. Depending upon your interests, this can either be a short stroll or a long half-day hike. The trail leads to eight different arches but also offers outstanding long-distance views of the La Sal Mountains, Bookcliffs to the north, and the Yellow Cat country to the northeast.

The first mile of trail is well defined to Landscape Arch, with short spurs to Pine Tree and Tunnel arches. Many walkers turn back at Landscape Arch, since the trail beyond is more challenging due to rocky terrain, slickrock slopes and narrow ledges with drop-offs on either side.

First described in an 1898 issue of *Science*, Landscape Arch is an incredible 306' span. In 1991, a visitor from Switzerland videotaped a chunk of the arch breaking loose and crashing to the desert floor, agents of erosion strike again!

From Landscape the trail continues to Double O Arch—with spurs to two other arches—Navajo and Partition. At Double O Arch, another one-way spur leads to Dark Angel, a free-standing spire. Hikers can return to the trailhead via the main trail or take the Primitive Loop back to Landscape Arch.

The Primitive Loop portion of the trail follows Fin Canyon downstream of Double O Arch, then cuts across a maze of sandstone fins and several small drainages before joining the main trail near Landscape Arch. A bit more challenging than the Landscape to Double O section, this trail is well worth the adventure. Be sure to watch for cairns that mark the trail.

Morning hikers may encounter mule deer grazing near the main trail. If you stand still, the deer may move closer for a better look. They are curious, not tame, and will bolt if you move suddenly.

In June, the does drop spotted fawns, sometimes bearing twins. Able to walk and run shortly after birth, the young will stay with their mothers in small groups. Though mountain lions prey on mule deer, sightings of the big cats in the park are rare.

DATURA

Nine miles north of Moab on U.S. 191 is the turnoff to Dead Horse Point State Park and Canyonlands National Park's Island In The Sky District. Turn west onto Utah 313, a Utah Scenic Byway, and continue fourteen miles to Dead Horse Point turnoff, then seven miles to the Visitor Center. The turnoff to the state park, dedicated in 1959, is well marked on Utah 313.

Dead Horse Point State Park is a prominent mesa that terminates in a sheer, narrow point. The exact naming behind the point is unclear, but many believe that turn-of-the-century ranchers rounded up wild horses that roamed the high mesas and herded them out onto this isolated and often waterless point. At The Neck, a large brush fence was constructed to corral these wild ponies. The cowboys cut out the desirable horses from the herds and left the unwanted or broomtails. Unfortunately, many died of thirst; hence, the name Dead Horse Point.

The State Park was designated in 1959 and consists of 5,200 acres. The sheer cliff walls of Wingate Sandstone are capped by the Kayenta Formation. Streams deposited the Kayenta Formation sediments in the Jurassic Period more than 160 million years ago, while the Wingate has wind-blown sands from a great Sahara-like environment.

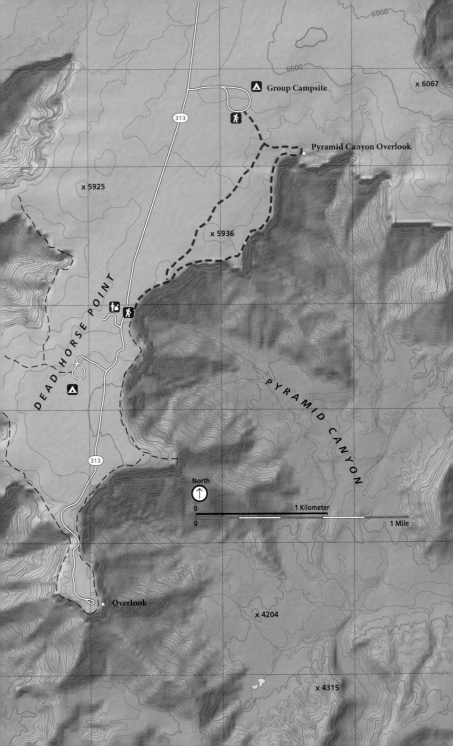

Group Campsite

313

Pyramid Canyon Overlook

x 6067

x 6000

x 5925

x 5936

DEAD HORSE POINT

PYRAMID CANYON

313

North

0

0   1 Kilometer

1 Mile

Overlook

x 4204

x 4315

31 Pyramid Canyon Overlook Trail

Trailhead: The Visitor Center or the Group Camping Site.
Mileage: A 3.75 mile-long loop trail.
Difficulty: Easy to Moderate.

From either trailhead, the Visitor Center or the Group Camping Site, hikers can follow this trail which parallels the rim of Pyramid Canyon and crosses through the grassland closer to the main road.

The Pyramid Canyon Overlook provides a vantage point into this wide canyon that drains to the Colorado River. Appropriately named, Pyramid Butte is visible in the distance, just south of the Shafer Trail road.

DESERT BIGHORN SHEEP

Desert bighorn live in this canyon. There is minimal disturbance from motorists or bikers, although old uranium prospecting roads do exist in the basin. The BLM constructed a wildlife guzzler, a man-made water collection system, in the upper reach of the canyon to provide a remote water source for the sheep. Native to Canyon Country, bighorn populations have declined regionally, due to diseases introduced from domestic livestock, hunting, habitat loss, and human disturbance.

Imagine what these grasslands looked like prior to settlement. There are old accounts of these grasses being "belly high to a horse."

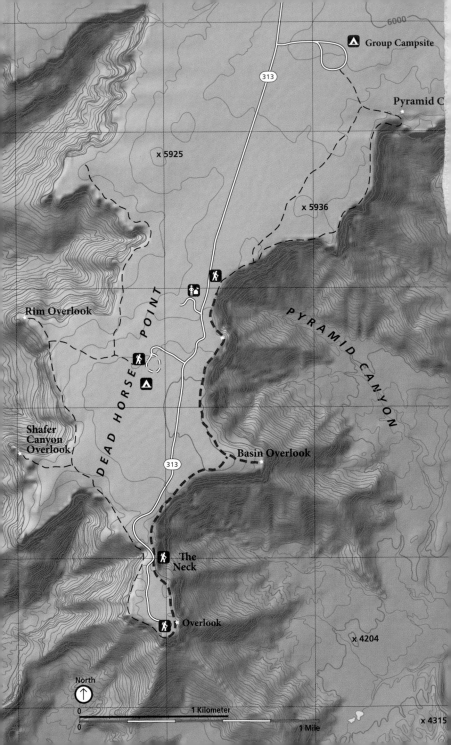

6000

▲ Group Campsite

313

Pyramid C

x 5925

x 5936

P Y R A M I D

Rim Overlook

DEAD HORSE POINT

C A N Y O N

Shafer
Canyon
Overlook

313

Basin Overlook

The
Neck

313

Overlook

x 4204

North
↑

0   1 Kilometer
0   1 Mile

x 4315

32 Basin Overlook and Point Overlook Trail

Trailhead: Visitor Center, The Neck, and Dead Horse Point Overlook.

Mileage: 2.0 miles one-way from the Visitor Center to Dead Horse Point Overlook, including the Basin Overlook spur. From the parking area at The Neck, there is a 1.0-mile loop trail to the main overlook.

Difficulty: Moderate.

This trail parallels the canyon rim from the Visitor Center to the Dead Horse Point Overlook. There are outstanding views of the La Sal Mountains, the evaporation ponds at the Potash Plant, and the Shafer Basin some 2,000 feet below. A short 0.25-mile spur trail branches off to the Basin Overlook.

From the Basin Overlook, one can see aptly named Pyramid Butte south of the evaporation ponds, and Chimney Rock, an isolated tower just north of the ponds. Rock climbers approach this tower by hiking up the Chinle talus slopes to the base of the Wingate cliff.

WINTER VIEW FROM DEAD HORSE POINT

During the late spring and summer, white-throated swifts may be observed zipping along these canyon rims hawking insects in flight. The narrow-winged birds appear to be dressed in tuxedos, their black back and wing feathers contrasting to the white throat and breast feathers. Built on small ledges located beneath exfoliating cliff faces, their rounded nests are made of grass and feathers glued together with swift spit.

Vegetation along this rim trail is typical of the pinyon-juniper woodlands, although you won't see many pinyon trees until you reach The Neck. Many of the dead trees along this trail resulted from a wildfire that probably started from a lightning strike. With a reduced tree canopy, smaller shrubs and grasses thrive. Blackbrush (*Coleogyne ramosissima*) is the many-branched shrub with linear leaves. Ramosissima means "many-branched," and the plants turn from gray to black when wet; hence, the common name. In spring these plants may wear a cloak of bright yellow flowers.

Remnants of an old pinyon-juniper fence exist at The Neck. You can see how easily the wild horses could be trapped out on the mesa. The original fence was much larger than the one that is here today.

At the Dead Horse Point Overlook there is a large shelter that provides shady relief from the sun; however this shelter is not a safe place to stand during electrical storms.

Group Campsite

Pyramid Canyon Overlook

313

x 5925

Big Horn
Overlook

x 5936

Rim Overlook

P
Y
R
A
M
I
D

C
A
N
Y
O
N

D
E
A
D

H
O
R
S
E

P
O
I
N
T

Shafer
Canyon
Overlook

Basin Overlook

313

The
Neck

Overlook

x 4204

x 4315

4600

x 4334

33 Shafer Canyon Overlook Trail

Trailhead: Dead Horse Point Overlook, The Neck, the Campground or the Visitor Center.

Mileage: From Dead Horse Point Overlook to the Campground, is a 2.5-mile one-way hike. Two spur trails, the Rim Overlook (0.25 miles one-way) and the Shafer Canyon Overlook (0.5 miles one-way) will add extra mileage to the length.

Difficulty: Easy. Be aware of cliff edges and sheer drop-offs.

A great trail for campers or day-hikers. Similar to other trails in the park, this route follows the rim of the East Fork of Shafer Canyon. Several spur trails lead to three overlooks: Meander Overlook (0.1 mile one-way), Shafer Canyon Overlook (0.5 mile one-way) and Rim Overlook (0.25 mile one-way). From these overlooks there are magnificent canyon and rock tower views in the East Fork of Shafer Canyon. Climbers ascend the isolated rock towers of Crows Head Spire (from Rim Overlook) and Bighorn Butte, which is also known as Birds View Butte (from Shafer Canyon Overlook). The White Rim Sandstone, a member of the Cutler Formation, is visible from the Rim Overlook. This sandstone forms the mezzanine level in the Island-in-the-Sky District of Canyonlands National Park, and is the namesake behind the White Rim Trail.

Along the Shafer Canyon Overlook trail, from the campground to the Meander Overlook, there are numerous pinyon pines (*Pinus edulis*) and Utah junipers (*Juniperus osteosperma*). The two-needled pinyons produce edible fruits—*edulis* means "edible"—and are sought after by wildlife and people. In contrast, the juniper has light-colored, scale-like leaves. The cones resemble bluish berries, but the waxy coating covers a hard shell and seed. Small rodents chisel these seed coats off and consume the small seeds. Infestations of the Ips beetle, along with prolonged drought conditions, have resulted in widespread pinyon die-offs throughout the Southwest.

Peregrine falcons nest beneath the canyon rim on this west side. The pair selects an overhanging ledge or small alcove for a nest site. These large falcons do not build a nest, rather they scrape a slight indentation in the soil in which their eggs will be laid. Fortunate visitors may observe these large falcons chasing down prey such as the white-throated swift or violet-green swallow in incredible aerial dogfights.

The trail up Shafer Canyon, in Canyonlands National Park, was used by the Ancestral Puebloans to access the mesa top. The Shafer brothers, Frank and J.H., along with W.J. Murphy, enlarged the trail in the early 1900s for their cattle and horses. This was a one-animal-wide trail—if a cow tried to turn around on the trail chances were it would fall over the edge—so the trail was enlarged in the 1950s for uranium exploration. The road building took one month to construct at a cost of approximately $20,000.

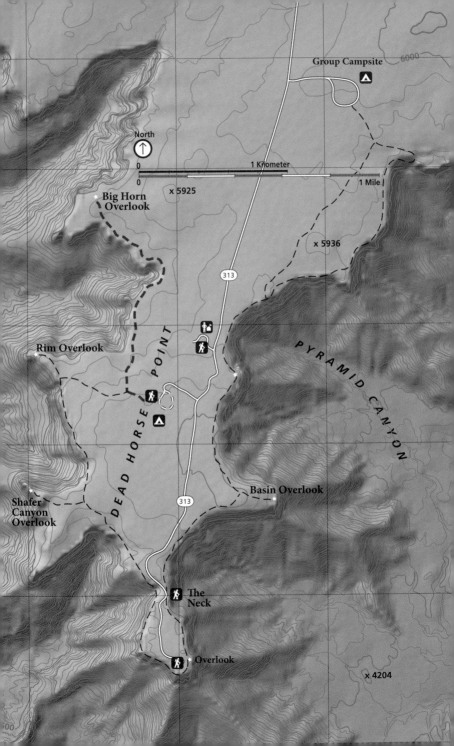

34 Big Horn Overlook

Trailhead: Campground or Visitor Center.
Mileage: 2.0 miles round-trip hike from the Campground, 2.5 miles round-trip hike from the Visitor Center.
Difficulty: Easy.

Another great walk, especially for campers. The trail follows the rim of Shafer Canyon's East Fork and ends at a series of potholes eroded into the Kayenta Sandstone, the cap rock above the cliff-forming Wingate Sandstone.

Water is a limiting factor in the desert. Take a dry, seemingly lifeless pothole, add rainwater or snowmelt, and soon the pool will teem with a vibrant, aquatic-rich universe. Pool size and water temperature are two factors that influence the aquatic species that will exist in these pools. In the smaller pools, there may be fairy shrimp, horsehair worms, midge larvae (called chironomids), and microscopic rotifers. The larger pools may have these in addition to tadpole shrimp, snails, dragonfly or damselfly nymphs, backswimmers, and clam shrimp.

Tadpole shrimp resemble two-inch-long horseshoe crabs, with their shield-shaped heads and long tails. Related more to extinct trilobites than salt-water shrimp, female tadpole shrimp may produce two types of eggs. The first set is produced under very favorable conditions and are almost all females. The second type, produced under less favorable conditions where temperature and oxygen levels in the pools may indicate overcrowding or drying conditions, are of both males and females. This second group are thick-walled eggs. The pools need to dry, then refill before the eggs hatch. This time period prevents premature hatching in shallow pools that will not hold water long enough for the tadpoles to mature.

Tiger Swallowtail

Water in the potholes attracts larger animals such as mule deer, bighorn sheep, coyotes, or birds. Ironically, amphibians such as the Great Basin spadefoot toad or the red-spotted toad may also be attracted to these pools. At night the red-spotted males will chorus, their drawn out trills sounding shrill in the night. The tadpoles of either species race through their life cycles before the ephemeral pool dries out, and the adults may burrow into the bottom of the pool to await the next breeding season.

The La Sal Mountains dominate the Moab skyline. Mount Peale, the highest peak in the range, stands at 12,721 feet. It was named for Dr. A.C. Peale, the geologist on the 1875 F.V. Hayden Geographical and Geological Survey. James Gardner and Henry Gannett led this survey, and the party mapped and explored the La Sals, which were known as the Elk Mountains back then. The most well known and most difficult to pronounce peak is Mount Tukuhnikivatz. Locally known as "Tuk," this volcanic-looking peak was named after a local Ute chief.

During the Escalante-Dominguez expedition of 1776, the cartographers recorded the "Sierra de la Sal" from the east side. The range was named for the salt flats along the flanks of the mountains where the Utes collected salt for trade, not because the Spaniards thought the peaks were capped by salt.

The La Sals are laccolithic in origin, meaning they formed from molten magma that cooled underground. The term is from the Greek words meaning "cistern" and "stone." Successive upward flows of magma intruded both vertically and laterally into the overlying layers of sedimentary rock, creating a "mushroom" of magma. This magma never erupted on the surface. During uplift of the entire Colorado Plateau, starting some 15 million years ago, the La Sals were thrust higher. Erosion wore away some of the sedimentary rock, and glaciers helped carve these rounded "blisters" of magma into the jagged mountain peaks of today. The remnants of these sedimentary layers are visible on the scree slopes high on the mountain's face.

With increased settlement in the Moab Valley, cattlemen and sheepherders turned to the mountains for summer forage. Though some of the local Utes and Paiutes were friendly with the settlers, conflicts arose.

Sometimes the winds of history swirl like a dust devil crossing open ground. The wind picks up pieces of dirt and debris like broken sentences and carelessly tosses them about like half-truths. The Pinhook Battle occurred in 1881 because two white men were killed on an outback ranch near the Colorado-Utah line. What precipitated the violence is unknown. A posse of miners and cowboys pursued the Indians, seeking revenge for the two ranchers. Accounts claim the posse was disorganized and ill prepared, while the Indians displayed impressive leadership and logistical tactics.

The parties collided in Pinhook Valley, on the northeast side of the La Sals. Seven of the posse and two locals from Moab were killed. Reports of Indian casualties varied between seven and eighteen dead. The Indians slipped away the following night. The dejected posse headed back to Colorado.

Later in the 1880s, gold seekers ventured into the mountains. Within a year's time, Miner's Basin was bustling with activity. Though the "bonanza" never materialized, miners continued to seek the Mother Lode.

President Teddy Roosevelt signed the La Sal Forest Reserve proclamation in 1906. This set aside a 158,000-acre reserve. Two blocks on the eastern bench of the La Sals were withdrawn prior to the establishment of the reserve. These blocks were granted in trust to the University of Utah and Utah State University and are currently managed by the Utah Division of Forestry, Fire and State Lands.

The early years of government management were difficult. Local resentment ran high and locals often clashed with the forest supervisor. Rudolph Mellenthin, a U.S. Forest Ranger nicknamed "the Kaiser," was killed in 1918 while trying to apprehend a World War One draft dodger. Mount Mellenthin (MELON-teen) is named after him.

In 1933, the Civilian Conservation Corp (CCC) landed in the La Sals. A camp was established at the Warner Ranger Station that spring. Crews built roads, trails, reservoirs, and water diversions as part of President Franklin Delano Roosevelt's New Deal.

Throughout the last 100 years, the La Sals have supported the local economic activities of Moab, La Sal,

Paradox, and other small communities. Grazing, timber harvesting, mining, oil and gas exploration, and recreation have all played roles in the history of this range. These activities are still underway today.

For hikers, the La Sals represent a cool respite from summer's heat. Though there are numerous trails in and around the La Sals (see José Knighton's book *La Sal Mountains: Hiking and Nature Handbook* for more detailed trail descriptions), this guide focuses on several hikes that start out near Oowah and Warner Lakes, as well as from the Geyser Pass Road. Also see the La Sal Mountain pamphlets by the Canyonlands Natural History Association.

Note: Elevations at Oowah and Warner Lakes are 8,780 and 9,400 feet, respectively. Be aware of your exertion at this higher elevation and pay attention to changing weather conditions.

Warner
Lake

Oowah Lake

Clark Lake

Haystack
Mountain

9000

9200

9400

9600

9800

10000

10200

10400

10600

10800

Horse Creek

Geyser Pass Road

Wet Fork Mil

H Creek

North

↑

0   1 Kilometer

0   1 Mile

35 Oowah Lake to Clark Lake

Trailhead: Oowah Lake.

Mileage: 1.5 miles to Clark Lake (one-way), 3.0 miles to Geyser Pass (one-way).

Difficulty: Moderate.

FALL COLOR ON TRAIL

Clark Lake was one of the CCC projects back in 1933. Though this is a nice destination for a hike, you might end up sharing it with livestock since it serves as a summer watering hole.

From Oowah Lake, the trail to Clark Lake climbs the slope via a series of switchbacks. During the summer months there may be numerous wildflowers that bloom along this trail. In turn, butterflies such as the painted lady, tiger swallowtail, Milbert's tortoiseshell, and others seek nectar from these flowers.

Black bears and mule deer may also be encountered along this trail. One day my family and I watched a mother black bear with her two cubs foraging near the trail. When she got a whiff of our scent, she snorted and the two cubs climbed right up two trees. A few minutes later she snorted again, and the two cubs came back down the trees. The family then wandered off into the forest.

At Clark Lake you have several choices. Continue upstream to Geyser Pass or return to Oowah Lake via the same trail or loop back to the lake via the Boren Mesa trail. The return via Boren Mesa is about 1.5 miles long.

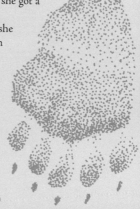

BEAR PRINT

The trail to Geyser Pass, named after pioneer cattleman Al Geyser, not for a waterspout, goes through aspen and spruce forests and some open meadows. Watch for forest birds like the Clark's nutcracker, red-breasted nuthatch, pine siskin, and blue grouse along this trail.

WILCOX
FLAT

Warner
Lake

Mill Creek

9000

Oowah Lake

BOREN MESA

North

0
0

1 Kilometer

1 Mile

9200

Clark Lake

9400

9600

9800

Horse Creek

Trailhead: Oowah Lake.
Mileage: 1.75 miles one-way.
Difficulty: Moderate.

From Oowah Lake, hike 0.4 mile down the main Oowah Lake Road to the Warner Lake trailhead or you could park and start from this point. Trail number 030 ascends through thickets of Gambel's oak, named in honor of William Gambel, a 19th century plant collector who died at the age of 28 in 1841.

Small in stature, these oaks provide a valuable food resource of acorns for mule deer, bears, rock squirrels, and jays. In spring and summer, these groves provide nesting habitat for orange-crowned warblers and green-tailed towhees.

The trail levels off and continues through aspen groves (called copses) to Warner Lake. Where the trail connects to a two-track, you could hike either way to reach Warner Lake. The left track continues to the ruins of the Warner Lake CCC Camp, established in 1933. In 1.1 mile, this track hits the Shafer Creek Trail, but continues towards the Warner Lake Road. The road junction is below Warner Lake, so follow the road up the hill to the lake.

The right track joins the Burro Pass Trail, which leads back to Warner Lake and the campground. There is another trail along Shafer Creek near this junction, but Warner Lake is about 100 yards north of this junction.

WARNER LAKE

Warner
Lake

Manns
Peak

Wet Fork Mill Creek

Burro Pass

North

0
1 Kilometer

0
1 Mile

Oowah Lake

Haystack
Mountain

9200

Clark Lake

9400

9600

Geyser Pass

9800

10000

10200

Geyser Pass Road

10400

10600

10800

37 Warner Lake to Burro Pass

Trailhead: Warner Lake Campground.
Mileage: 3.25 miles (one-way).
Difficulty: Moderate although the trail is steep in places.

This is a great summer hike that originates at Warner Lake and winds through aspen and spruce forests to a high elevation vista of the La Sals.

From the campground, hike towards Warner Lake, pass through the pole fence built to keep cattle out of the campground, and follow the main trail past the junctions with the Shafer Creek and Warner Lake trails.

Keep an eye out for mule deer, elk, black bears, and the numerous birds that inhabit these forests. Broad-tailed hummingbirds may be present, feeding on nectar, while Cordilleran flycatchers feed on aerial insects. Listen for the high-pitched whistles of pikas, small rodents that live in the rocky avalanche or scree slopes. The La Sal pika, a species endemic to these mountains, forages for grasses and forbs throughout the day. The small mammals pile the vegetation in small haystacks under protected ledges for winter forage.

MULE DEER

Like many of the mountain trails, this one may have a profusion of wildflowers. Columbine, sneezeweed, lupine, and asters create a mosaic of color along the trail.

Mount Tomasaki, visible from Burro Pass to the east, is named for one of the Paiute guides accompanying the Hayden Survey party.

38 Warner Lake to Gold Knob and Miner's Basin

Trailhead: Warner Lake Campground or Miner's Basin.
Mileage: 1.75 miles (one-way) to Gold Knob.
Difficulty: Moderate.

It is a steep climb up Schuman Gulch to reach Gold Knob, but it is well worth the effort. There are spectacular views of the surrounding peaks and desert below from this vantage point.

To reach the trailhead, hike down the road from the Warner Lake Campground about 100 yards to the sign. The trail starts in a thick grove of aspens and soon passes nearby to an enclosed spring, then starts to climb through subalpine fir (*Abies lasiocarpa*) and Engelmann spruce (*Picea engelmannii*). One difference between the two is the feel of the needles. The prickly spruce needles are a sharp contrast to the softer subalpine fir ones. Also, spruce cones hang downwards, while those of the fir are upright on the branches.

The ruin of a cabin heralds back to the era when miners prospected for gold and silver in these mountains.

After the switchbacks up the gulch, the trail crosses a wide open slope. The small summit to the west is Gold Knob. Named for the autumn coloration of golden aspens, this viewpoint is reached by taking the 0.5-mile spur trail that branches off of the main trail. This spur starts just past a stand of tall spruce trees.

One option to hiking back down the slope to Warner Lake is to continue over the divide into Miner's Basin. This route can also be hiked in reverse from the trailhead in Miner's Basin.

Warner Lake to Gold Knob & Miner's Basin, La Sal Mountains 127

WILCOX FLAT

SCHUMAN GULCH

×11152

× 1

Warner Lake

× 10715

Mill Creek

9000

Oowah Lake

BOREN MESA

Hays
Moun

× 9089

9200

Clark Lake

× 9394

9400

9600

Horse Creek

9800

10000

10200

Geyser Pass Road

10400

North

0
1 Kilometer

0
1 Mile

10600

Trans La Sal Trail – Oowah Lake to Geyser Pass Road

Trailhead: Geyser Pass Road, 3.1 miles from junction with La Sal Mountain Loop Road.
Mileage: 2.5 miles one-way.
Difficulty: Moderate to Difficult.

The Trans La Sal Trail skirts the west side of the range. Though there are various options to this trail, including backpacking the entire length, the description below is for the segment between Oowah Lake and the Geyser Pass Road. This trail is also known as the Boren Mesa Trail. You can hike out and back from either Oowah Lake or the parking lot along the Geyser Pass Road, or set up a shuttle between these two points. Several loop options also exist.

From Oowah Lake, the trail crosses the earthen dam, then climbs out of the drainage. You will pass by quaking aspen (*Populus tremuloides*) and Douglas fir (*Pseudotsuga menziesii*) trees. The powdery coating on the aspen bark easily rubs off, and makes for some fun face painting. Whenever a slight wind sets the long-stemmed leaves to rustling, this tree's names are evident—tremuloides which means "trembling" or "quaking." Aspens reproduce by seed or root sucker. The long, lateral root systems send up shoots or suckers. This characteristic enables these trees to quickly recolonize a site after a major disturbance like a fire or an avalanche.

Douglas fir trees have soft needles arranged in a whorled pattern and pointed red buds. The cone has a three-lobed bract that extends from beneath the scales. One tale explains how a mouse seeking safety from a great forest fire ran up the Douglas fir trunk and hid beneath the cone's scales. Of course, the mouse didn't fit, and today you can still see its tail and two legs sticking out from beneath the scale.

Follow the tree blazes that mark this trail. There are several cattle paths, four-wheel-drive roads and bike trails that cross this one, lending some confusion to the route. Continue past the connecting trail to Clark Lake, and pass through intermittent clearings and groves of aspen to the top of Boren Mesa.

The mesa is named after Carl Boren, who was a pioneer cattleman and settled in the area around 1876.

From Boren Mesa the trail drops off into the Horse Creek drainage, but not before a fine vantage of the Mill Creek gorge. Continue downslope to a crossing of Horse Creek, then climb upward out of the drainage. By-pass a four-wheel-drive road that intercepts the trail, and keep heading southwest to the parking area/pullout on the Geyser Pass Road.

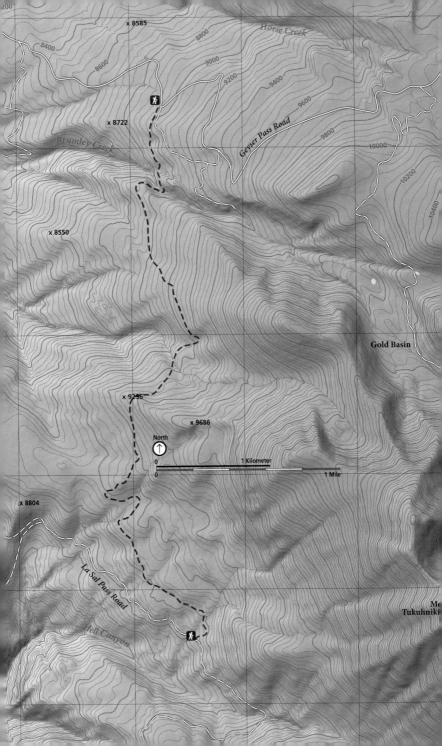

40 Trans La Sal Trail – Geyser Pass Road to La Sal Pass Road

Trailhead: On the Geyser Pass Road, 3.2 miles from junction with La Sal Mountain Loop Road.

Mileage: 3.75 miles one-way.

Difficulty: Moderate to Difficult.

This is another segment of the Trans La Sal Trail that utilizes the parking area/pullout on the Geyser Pass Road. The trail goes south from this pullout to the La Sal Pass Road. The change in elevation is not as great as the segment between Geyser Pass and Oowah Lake.

The trail passes through groves of Gambel's oaks and quaking aspens. In fall the oak leaves change color and may exhibit a mosaic of color. During the shorter days, the leaf's chlorophyll pigments start to break down and the secondary pigments are unveiled. Acorns are important fall food resources for wildlife.

The aspen groves attract numerous species of birds, notably woodpeckers that excavate cavities in the soft trunks of the trees. Any abandoned holes do not go vacant for very long, as house wrens, mountain bluebirds, mountain chickadees, and other wildlife utilize these cavities for their nest locations.

Keep an eye out for Colorado columbine (*Aquilegia caerulea*) that blooms in the shadows of these aspens. The large white or bluish flowers attract

hummingbirds that pollinate the flowers in return for nectar. Also be aware of stinging nettles (*Urtica dioica*), a tall plant with square-shaped stems and opposite leaves with saw-toothed edges. The stems bear numerous stinging hairs that, when broken, secrete formic acid.

The trail crosses Brumley Creek, a cold mountain stream named after the owner of a sawmill in Gold Basin. Farther along, the trail crosses Dorry Creek, named after Dorry Crouse, a pioneer sheepherder.

COLORADO COLUMBINE
Aquilegia caerulea

Past Dorry Creek, the trail goes through forests of fir and aspen, and glades of oaks and shrubs. As the trail approaches Hell Canyon it will connect with a two-track from the La Sal Pass Road. Follow this track past small meadows, and a cabin and spring at Squaw Spring to reach the main road.

Area Information Sources

Canyonlands Natural History
Association
3031 S. Hwy 191
Moab, UT 84532
435-259-6003
www.cnha.org

Moab Information Center
Center and Main
Moab, UT 84532

Moab Area Travel Council
84 North 100 East
Moab, UT 84532
435-259-1370
www.discovermoab.com

Bureau of Land Management
Moab Field Office
82 East Dogwood
Moab, UT 84532
435-259-2100
www.blm.gov/utah/moab.html

Sand Flats Recreation Area
125 E. Center St.
Moab, UT 84532
435-259-2444
www.grandcountyutah.net/sandflats/
index.htm

Canyon Country Museum of Moab
(Dan O'Laurie Canyon Country
Museum)
118 E. Center St.
Moab, UT 84532
435-259-7985

Manti La Sal National Forest
Moab Ranger District
62 E. 100 N.
Moab, UT 84532
435-259-7155
www.fs.fed.us/r4/mantilasal/

Arches National Park
P.O. Box 907
Moab, UT 84532
435-719-2299
www.nps.gov/arch

Fiery Furnace
and camping reservations:
www.Recreation.gov

Canyonlands National Park
2282 S. West Resource Blvd
Moab, UT 84532
435-719-2313
www.nps.gov/cany

The Nature Conservancy
Scott M. Matheson Wetlands Preserve
P.O. Box 1329
Moab, UT 84532
435-259-4629
www.nature.org/wherewework/
northamerica/states/utah/preserves

Dead Horse Point State Park
P.O. Box 609
Moab, UT 84532-0609
435-259-2614
1-800-322-3770 *Camping Reservations*
www.stateparks.utah.gov/parks/
mapping/deadhorse/area.htm